LETTING BLAKE GO

What really happened between
Blake Fielder-Civil and Amy Winehouse

LETTING
BLAKE GO

What really happened between
Blake Fielder-Civil and Amy Winehouse

GEORGETTE CIVIL
With John McDonald

APEX PUBLISHING LTD

First published in 2014 by
Apex Publishing Ltd
12A St. John's Road, Clacton on Sea, Essex, CO15 4BP, United Kingdom

www.apexpublishing.co.uk

British Library Cataloguing-in-Publication Data
A catalogue record for this book
is available from the British Library

ISBN 978-1-908382-61-0
1-908382-61-9

Typeset in 10.5pt Baskerville Win95BT

Editor: Kim Kimber
Production Manager: Chris Cowlin
Cover Design: Hannah Blamires

Printed and bound by
Berforts Printers, Kings Lynn, Norfolk

Publishers Note:
The views and opinions expressed in this publication are those of the author and are not necessarily those of Apex Publishing Ltd

Copyright:
Every attempt has been made to contact the relevant copyright holders, Apex Publishing Ltd would be grateful if the appropriate people contact us on: 01255 428500 or mail@apexpublishing.co.uk

For my boys

CONTENTS

CHAPTER 1
A PHONE CALL –
A SUICIDE PACT

The telephone rang on 23rd July 2010. It had been a good day for me, even though the salon was gone – it seemed like a weight off my shoulders. I'd decided to change direction and work with ex-offenders.

'Hi Georgette.'

'Hi.'

'I have some bad news.'

'Oh no .. is it Blake?'

'It's Amy. Amy is dead.'

I couldn't believe what I was hearing – Amy? Dead? I could hardly breath. I knew I had to ring the prison. Tears began to flow. I repeated her name, over and over. Maybe it was a joke, maybe someone was just having me on. But why would anyone do such a cruel thing?

I called the prison, but they wouldn't let me talk to Blake. They said the Governor would call me back – which he did.

'Don't worry, Blake is in the best place.'

'Is he?'

'He's on suicide watch.'

'Can I come see him?'

'No. Better if he's left alone for now.'

I'd heard that before, many times over the past few years. But I suppose they were right, he couldn't harm himself in there – or could he? I thought to myself, if Amy's dead, Blake will be next. My heart went out to the Winehouse family, I could only imagine what they were going through right then.

As the tragedy began to sink in, my mind went back, to another phone call that changed my life, less than three years earlier – on Friday 9th November 2007.

It was just a normal day – before that previous telephone call. Life was going on as usual. Well, as usual as was possible, under the circumstances – Blake had the GBH charge hanging over his head, but we weren't worried. We thought we had that sorted. I went off to work as usual at Salon 54, my hairdressing business in Ruskington, Lincolnshire. I chatted to the girls, Tracy and Pam, about the usual things – you know, the weather, families, plans for the weekend, gossip – commonplace things – everyday things. We had cooked chicken and rolls for lunch, Tracy's favourite, and it was my turn to pay. It was Friday, and we always had a Baileys after work on Fridays and a laugh and a giggle – you know, ordinary kind of things. Then I drove home to Cromwell Cottage, in Barnby Lane, Claypole, a small village in Lincolnshire, where I lived. On the surface, a very average and normal kind of place – before it became the Village of the Damned.

It was late when Amy rang me. I can't remember the precise time – not now. I could remember for a long time after that night. A long time – the precise time she rang. But I can't remember now, not after everything that's happened since then.

The evening before, Amy had telephoned more than usual. She kept telling me that her father, Mitch Winehouse, wanted her to go to dinner with him. He wasn't in the habit of taking her to dinner and she asked me what she should do. It was a strange question to ask, but she sounded a bit wasted, so I didn't pay much attention. I was anxious to know where Blake was and she said he was with some friends. I asked her if he was alright and she assured me he was. Five minutes later she telephoned again and we had the same conversation.

'Where is Blake, Amy?'

'He's with friends, momsie.'

This happened several more times and we had the conversation several more times. I was getting a little anxious by now. Something was happening and I didn't know what it was.

'Don't go with your dad yet, Amy, let me ring Blake first.'

'Dad's being insistent.'

It was the first time I'd ever heard Amy call Mitch "dad" and that was strange in itself. But I only became really worried when she said her "sailor", which was the nickname she gave Blake, would never be taken away from her, no matter how much it cost. That made alarm bells ring. Why would she say that? We had everything sorted – didn't we?

'I'm going to ring Blake, Amy.

'Please don't say anything, momsie. It's not safe ..'

'I thought everything was taken care of?'

She rang off, as if someone had interrupted her. I was afraid to call Blake, afraid of what he might say to me – or what he might not be able to say to me. So I asked Giles to do it instead. Giles said I was being paranoid, but he didn't know about the warning I'd had. He didn't know about my meeting with the strange and threatening René Butler, who I believed to be a drug-dealer, at the salon a couple of days earlier – and the cryptic message I had been given for Blake. The sketch which the enigmatic René drew for me flashed into my mind and I panicked a bit.

'Please Giles .. I'm so worried!'

Giles eventually did as I asked and telephoned Blake.

'Hi Blake, are you OK?'

'Sure, Daydreams, I'm with some friends.'

'Mum's worried. She's had Amy on the phone, Mitch wants to take her to dinner.'

'Don't worry, Daydreams, everything's OK. Tell mum I love her.'

Giles told me not to worry, it was just Amy being Amy.

So I relaxed.

But that was the day before – that was Thursday 8th November 2007. This was the day after, this was Friday 9th November 2007. The phone rang again. It was Amy again.

'Momsie, I've got something to tell you .. you mustn't worry. Promise.'

'What is it, Amy?'

'Promise, momsie ..'

'I promise!'

'Blake's been arrested.'

I could hear Mitch Winehouse's voice in the background – distant, matter-of-fact.

'Do you think I should ring Georgette, Amy?'

'I'm doing it, dad.'

I was really panicking now. I could hear the fear in my own voice. I could taste the apprehension. It was as if I knew something really bad had happened, something that had been waiting to happen and had now, finally, manifested itself.

'Amy .. what do you mean arrested? Why? What are you talking about?'

I asked Amy these questions, but I already knew the answers. I knew what had happened. I had been told – warned. I ignored the warning and now I was facing the consequences, the unthinkable aftermath. Amy's voice came back down the telephone line.

'Please don't worry, momsie. He'll be home soon. He's OK. It's the King thing .. you know .. King'

I knew, but I wasn't listening. I was already making plans – the plans I should have made earlier. Of course I knew it was the King thing, she didn't have to tell me. She didn't have to explain. Her voice sounded shaky on the phone – off-beat, hesitant.

'He's been charged with conspiracy. I'm with Alex .. at Stratford.'

'When did this happen?'

'Yesterday, last night .. earlier today .. I'm not sure ..'

'Why did you take so long to call me?'

I was shouting into the phone. Yesterday? I knew it! The feeling I had yesterday evening was right – that something was wrong. Something was going wrong! The phone was strangely quiet at the other end. There was no explanation as to why it had taken more than twenty-four hours for me to be told that my son had been arrested.

I shouted into the phone again.

'We're on our way!'

Life can be a strange thing. It can be wonderful one minute, it can be terrible the next. "Wonderful", "terrible" – they're only words – interchangeable, as the circumstances of life dictate. Words – like "suicide", a word that can be terrible – would be terrible to most people. But it can be wonderful too. It can be wonderful to someone who has nothing left to live for. It's a word that can bring peace and sleep, where there was no peace nor sleep before.

This is how I felt, less than two years after that fateful phone call.

Giles had left me by then and I was just wandering round the house at rock-bottom – frightened, confused, shell-shocked, not sleeping or eating.

'You're depressed, darling.'

Giles said those words before he went.

'I love you very much .. always have, always will. But you can't go on like this. You need to see a doctor.'

I cried silent tears every night, so the boys wouldn't hear me. I prayed that I wouldn't jeopardise Blake's recovery. He was already angry at Giles and I didn't want to burden him with my depression. I turned Giles' words over and over in my head – over and over. I knew he was right, I was sinking deeper and deeper into my own hell. I was being consumed by hatred for everything and everybody – except my boys.

I read tabloid reports of Amy drinking, fighting, getting wasted most of the time – and, whether they were true or not, it was always Blake's fault, even though he wasn't there and had no control over what she was doing. They called him a "junkie". What an ugly word for a mother to hear being shouted at her son – constantly, never-ending, repeated and repeated and repeated. It filled me with horror. Everybody had a dreadful opinion of Blake. Everybody believed he was the devil incarnate and the worst of the peddlers perpetuated that image to sell their lies. Those with most to hide themselves screamed it loudest. Yet nobody knew him – took the time to know him – really knew him, like I did.

'Idiots!'

I would scream this back at the unhearing ears.

'How dare you! That's my son!'

Yet it continued, day in and day out.

'Junkie loser!'

'He destroyed Amy!'

I cared about Amy. Of course I cared about Amy, I cared very deeply. But I loved Blake and I couldn't do much to save Amy. I knew this, because I'd tried and failed.

People stood outside my house and stared in through the windows.

'That's where the junkie's mother lives.'

The boys got it at school too. One of Harry's teachers called Amy a "manbeast", whatever that means, and grown people would look at Fred and sneer.

'You're just like your junkie brother.'

How could so-called Christian people say that to a child? Was it any wonder he was getting into trouble? And the people in the village – they tried to be polite and hide behind hypocrite smiles. But I could always see that word behind their eyes.

'Junkie!'

I would rant at Giles in my depression and hatred. I would scream terrible things in my pain and frustration – things that were beneath me. I know that now, but at the time there was no other outlet, no other safety valve, no other way of ending the terrible, terrible darkness in my heart. I screamed words like "cowards" and "gutless" and "ugly" and "shallow" and "stupid" and "dirty" and –

'How would they like it if I called them fat, or horrible, or drunken, or self-righteous, or bigoted?"

I ranted all this at Giles and he listened, over and over and over, to me shouting and crying and feeding my hatred. My son would always be judged. Forever. And so would I. Poor Giles, he listened. And he was right, I did need to see a doctor. But how can you tell a doctor about the agony inside you? It's not a physical thing, it has no outward signs, apart from the emotional ones. How can you explain your anger to someone who can never understand, who has probably pre-judged you like all the others and who doesn't really care whether you live or die – like your junkie son!

That's when I first thought about suicide. I tried not to think about it. I hid it away at the back of my mind, where I couldn't see it. But I knew it was there. I pretended it wasn't, but I knew it was. The thought terrified me. I would have conversations with myself in bed at night, as if I were two people at once – schizophrenic – one voice calm and reasonable and the other dark and seductive. I would get up and pace round the house, my voices arguing with each other.

'Stop these thoughts!'

6

'Why are you crying?'
'I don't know.'
'Have a coffee.'
'I should ring mum.'
'It's too late.'
'Why can't I sleep?'
'You know why.'
'Don't make me think it.'
'You want to kill yourself and your children.'
'No!'
'Yes!'
'I can't kill my children.'
'You can't leave them behind you.'
'Please stop! Stop! Stop! I'm so tired .. tired and frightened.'

Tired and frightened. Frightened and tired of it all. I wanted to sleep, but sleep just would not come. The house itself was becoming a strange place to me – somewhere I once knew, but could no longer recognise. I felt so desperately alone. Only someone who has been completely alone, while surrounded by people, can know how I felt. It seemed to me that, wherever I went, I would be judged for my sins. I would not be judged impartially, nor objectively, but according to the rules of the culture that my beloved son had dragged me into. I longed to hear Blake's voice. I wanted his reassurance. But he'd been taken away and I no longer had access to the reality of him, only to the unreality – the false reality. The sadness in the house weighed me down like a heavy dark blanket. It frightened me, like an entity that was outside myself but still part of myself, nevertheless. It was a devil to whom I wished I could sell my soul, if it could bring back the happiness – that time when we were all together and happy. I would do anything for that, to have that time back again.

Then, one particularly lonely night, I made myself a coffee and Baileys and took it to bed with me. I knew the coffee wouldn't help, but maybe the Baileys would. The house felt so dark and cold without Blake and Giles. I remember stopping at the top of the stairs and listening to Harry and Fred breathing. At least they were able to sleep. The house frowned at me, growled at me. It knew I hated it now, having loved it once-upon-a-time. I went to my room and sipped my coffee and Baileys under the duvet, without turning the lights on. I could see the shape of the window, the shape of the mirror, the shape of the furniture – the shapes seemed to be converging, closing in on me. Closing me in! I shut my eyes tight and allowed my mind to drift back over the months that had passed – since that phone call.

I knew I was at the end. It was all over. I could go no further. There was no light – there would be no more light.

But there was a way to find peace – and sleep. I held it in my own hands. I'd hid it away in that place at the back of my mind, where I couldn't see it. But I knew it was still there, waiting for the right time, and now I looked at it. I could do it now, as long as the boys came with me. I found myself speaking out loud in the darkness – in the room – in the hostile house.

'Oh Lord, I am so very sorry. I know you will understand, I have no choice. I can't stand this misery and pain any longer.'

As soon as I'd said it, acknowledged it, I experienced an overwhelming sense of relief.

'The boys and I are coming to you, Lord. Please help me to make the journey as painless as possible.'

The house growled, the shadows danced around me, the world outside the window laughed and pointed its accusing finger. But I didn't care. Nothing could get to me now – now that I'd made the decision.

'I'll wait for Blake to come home, then I'll do it. I'll kill myself and my boys .. my beautiful boys.'

But how would I do it? I'd shoot us – no, too bloody, the boys were too beautiful for that. Poison? But, would it work? Would it be slow and cruel? I decided to postpone the physical process of suicide. It would come to me – the means – the method. The perfect way. As long as the decision was finally made, that's all that mattered for now. Tomorrow would be a happy day again, at last – a day nearer to our journey – to when we would fly together, away from this place.

For the first time in what seemed like a lifetime, I felt a peacefulness envelop me, a warmth, as if God had wrapped me in his arms. And I dreamt of Blake and Fred and Harry and me – we were holding hands and flying through the sky, like the children in Peter Pan. We could see the stars – they were dark and light at the same time. Sparking. Winking at us. Laughing with us like excited school-kids when the summer break comes round. It was so, so amazing.

'Look at us, mum, we're flying!'

'Yes, my darlings, we are. We're together and we're free!'

I began to cry. I'm not sure why.

CHAPTER 2
BLAKE – THE DEMON

I hung up the phone after speaking to Amy and immediately began to hyperventilate. I was filled with foreboding. Conspiracy? Oh no! I knew this would happen. I should have listened to the warning. I should have done something about it. But what? And what the hell were we going to do now? Giles and I argued, with me shouting and him trying to make me see reason and saying there was nothing we could do at this time of night and we should wait until morning.

'No!'

I screamed. Panic and fear filled me – fear and panic and dread.

'We must go now. I have to be near him.'

Blake would know I'd come to him, he would be waiting for me. But they hadn't told me till now – he'd been arrested yesterday and they hadn't told me until today. He would have been waiting all that time, not knowing that I didn't know. We had an hour until the last train into Kings Cross. Enough time. God knows what we were going to do when we got there, to London. But I didn't care, I just had to be near him. I hoped it wasn't as bad as I thought. I hoped I was over-reacting. I hoped we could get it all sorted out by tomorrow and Blake would be back home.

I was in a kind of shocked state, I suppose, as I boarded the train at Newark. At such short notice, we had no alternative but to take our other sons, Harry and Fred, with us. Harry was almost fifteen at the time and Fred was thirteen. Understandably, Giles didn't want to involve them, but what could I do? Giles and I continued to argue, all the way to the station, with the boys worried by our side. Then silence overtook us – once we were on the train and it began to move – a resigned calmness on the outside, even though there was turmoil inside. We sat in our seats and thought our separate thoughts, as the train sped through the night towards London. I don't know what Giles was thinking, nor can I say what was going through Harry's and Fred's minds – poor boys.

My head was full of Blake.

I met Lance Fielder several lifetimes before my decision to commit suicide. I was on the rebound from a failed engagement to someone else and totally devastated. My friends took me out one night to cheer me up and I met Lance. It all happened so very quickly after that and some of it is opaque to me now – cloudy – through a glass darkly. Before I knew what was happening, Lance picked me up from work one Monday with a marriage licence and I was thrown off my feet – it all seemed so glamorous – so exciting – so chic – so very sophisticated.

'Marry me right now!'

He was eighteen years older than me and very persuasive, so I did – marry him. Right then! My parents were furious and never really came to terms with it. Maybe it was because they wanted the full wedding formalities for me, their little "titch", as they used to call me, because of my size. Or maybe it was something to do with Lance – something they sensed. Maybe they knew it wouldn't work, because they were older, had more experience and more sense than I had. I don't know. I only know that, if that's what it was, then they were right. It didn't work. It couldn't work.

It turned out that Lance Fielder wasn't the gallant gentleman I believed him to be, at least not to me, and it didn't take me very long to realise that I had made a mistake. He bullied me and was nasty and controlling. He was also very jealous of my family, to whom I was extremely close, and he wanted to hurt them by denying them any contact with me. He mimicked my mum's Belgian accent and made fun of my dad. Mutual acquaintances told me that Lance had been violent to his previous wife and I was constantly afraid that he would, eventually, become violent to me.

Shortly after our marriage, Lance told me he was going to sell our home in Moulton, Northampton, to buy a restaurant in Javea. I didn't know where Javea was, but I soon found out it was in Spain, and we were going to move over there to live. I was pregnant with Blake and I didn't want to go. But Lance was a man who was used to getting what he wanted – so it was pointless to argue. I had to go. Maybe if I hadn't been pregnant, I would have put up more of a fight – maybe. But I was pregnant, and this was a source of great joy to me, an anaesthetic that blocked out reality and made me so happy, a happiness that was inside myself, away from the outside and the rest of it – the nastiness of the rest of it. I was going to be a mother and I was so internally happy!

So I went.

Lance didn't improve in Spain. He had affairs with other women in Javea, while I was pregnant – one was a young fourteen-year-old girl who worked for us in the bar. One day she just left, without giving any reason, confirming to me that the attraction had been one-sided and that perhaps Lance had forced his affections upon her – maybe threatening to sack her if she didn't comply. Her father came to me and asked what had happened. How could I tell him? How could I disillusion the man and destroy his daughter's reputation? So I said I didn't know – even though I did.

Lance continued to frequent brothels with a variety of his dubious associates and I was worried about the effect all this might have on my unborn son, when the boy finally came into the world and began to grow up.

Little did I know!

All the time, Blake's birth was getting closer. And I was so alone – we were so alone, my precious unborn son and I – in Spain. It was a loneliness that pervaded every moment of the day and night for me. I didn't know what to do, but my parents insisted that the baby should be born in the UK for citizenship reasons and, to my great relief, Lance agreed with them for once. So, in February 1982, I returned to Mears Ashby, Northampton, where they lived, and stayed there until Blake was born, on 16th April. It was fabulous to be home, being with mum and dad, being looked after and spoilt by them. I loved it, after the isolation and desolation of Spain.

My mother and father were at my side when I went into labour. Lance wasn't. But it was an easy birth and the moment I held my little Blake in my arms, I felt that nothing could ever hurt me again. I have never, ever experienced such love, like the love I felt for Blake on that late evening in April 1982. My little son was so perfect – so beautiful.

Lance and I were finished, I knew that, but now I had my little Blake and that was all I needed. Nobody had ever felt the way I did that night – as least that's what I believed. I'm sure that many other mothers felt that way, but to me, then – right then – nobody felt like me. Nobody was as happy as me. Nobody was as lucky as me. Nobody was a mother like me. Nobody!

I spent a further month with my parents, after Blake was born, before going back to Javea. I tried to put it off, but I knew I would have to go back to Spain eventually. I felt so guilty, because I knew I was going back to end the marriage. I mean, how can you have a child, then almost immediately take his father away from him? I was in turmoil – any decision I made would affect Blake for the rest of his life. But it felt right, I felt I was doing the right thing. The mother's instinct inside me told me it was the right thing. It's frightening, even now, after everything that's happened, I still feel that emotion, that sense of protectiveness. Like Lady Macduff with her little son – her "poor bird". And the wren she spoke of, "the most diminutive of birds", a titch like me, who "fights against the owl to protect her nest".

But I know I have to let it go.

I went back to Spain with Blake, when he was six weeks old. I cried hysterically at the airport, hugging my father, desperate not to go. But it was something I had to do. I had to do it, because I believed I owed Lance that much at least. Alright, it was a mistake to marry him. It was my fault. But I was unhappy at the time and it seemed like the right thing to do. How many people have felt like that – at the time – felt they were doing the right thing, at the time, only to regret it soon after? When you're young and you've been hurt and you feel the world is against you, it's easy to fall in love – or to think you're in love, when you're really just looking for a shoulder, any shoulder. It's easy. People tell you afterwards what a fool you've been and you agree with them and you ask yourself how you could have been such a fool – but it's easy. Everybody knows it's easy.

Lance didn't want me to leave him – I don't know why. I assumed he wanted Blake, his son, but he really only wanted to have his own way. It took me a while to get away from him, after I went back over to Javea. He would tell me I couldn't go, he wouldn't allow it. He would hold Blake in the air, over his head, and shout to me.

'You want him? Come and get him!'

'Please, Lance ..'

'You can't have your son!'

'Please, Lance, don't ..'

I would be physically sick with worry, in case he might hurt my baby, who was only four months old at the time. I realised that Lance was using Blake as a weapon, to keep me under control and to keep my family away. Why he would want to keep me there against my will, I don't know. It was probably something to do with his psyche – he was a man who didn't like people getting one over on him, and he probably thought my leaving would be a victory for me in some way and a defeat for him. In the end, I couldn't take it any longer and I made my getaway furtively and silently, in the night, in the shadows, taking nothing with me, except my beloved little son.

It was like coming out of the dark, into the light, when I returned from Spain. Back to the love – away from the hate. Blake was surrounded by love then – when we came back from Javea. I loved him and my family loved him – my mum would spend hours reading to him and my dad taught him the names of every bird that perched in the garden. There was just so much affection around my son. I bought our first house and we settled together, happy and secure with each other, in our little world. How can a person go wrong, when they're surrounded by so much love?

I know how. Now.

Lance followed us back to England, at least I believe he followed us. Fourteen months after I left, he sold the restaurant and bought a go-kart track in Leicester. He came to see Blake, he said it was his right. I resented his visits, because I knew he was only doing it to get back at me and my family – asserting his rights, not loving his son. And the visits never went well, he constantly made fun of my family and me and said such cruel things to Blake. I took the matter to court, but the court granted Lance weekend access, every two weeks. Long before each visit,

Blake would begin to get worried, hiding behind chairs and trying to make himself sick in the bathroom, hoping he wouldn't have to go. As he grew older, he became more and more anxious. It made me anxious as well, but there was nothing I could do about it. Was there?

Blake was treated roughly by Lance, who would make him spend the entire weekend at the go-kart track and he'd come home tired, dirty and hungry. He was never allowed to telephone me, even to say goodnight. It almost broke my heart, every time I had to let him go.

'Don't you want to go, darling?'

'Only if you come, mummy.'

'I can't, my darling. I can't.'

'Then I won't go either.'

'You must. You must ..'

I complained to Lance, that he was making his son very unhappy. I would tell him that Blake didn't want to visit him and ask him why couldn't he leave us alone. But he would just sneer at me. He would laugh at me.

'Stop making such a fuss!'

'I'm worried about Blake, Lance.'

'You worry too much about that boy. You dance round him too much!'

'You're cruel to him!'

'You spoil him!'

And that's the way it would go. I had met Giles by now and, eventually, we found out that Lance and his various girlfriends would often be naked when Blake was there. They would be in the bath together, or walking round the house naked, or even behaving in a sexually explicit manner. Lance would leave Blake in the care of his girlfriends and his dubious associates, people Blake didn't know – people I didn't know, when he wasn't there. I immediately stopped the visits and went back to court. It took the legal system an age to come to its decision, and Lance fought me every step of the way. Finally, the lawyers and welfare people wanted to speak to Blake, to hear what he had to say, behind closed doors. Blake didn't want to talk to them.

'Do I have to, mummy?'

'Be brave, my darling, you'll be safe.'

After a series of these meetings, the judge decided he needed to speak to Blake alone, so he took my son into his chambers. We waited, Giles and I – Lance and his barrister. After what seemed like a lifetime, Blake came out – he looked sad and confused. The judge ruled that all further access be denied to Lance, who was granted letters, school reports and photographs. Nothing else. The court decided that it wasn't in Blake's best interest to see Lance again, but the boy should keep the name "Fielder" – which is still on his passport. I was so relieved. We could go home now, my son and I, and we'd never be separated again.

I never did find out what Blake spoke to the judge about – until it was too late.

Some time later, however, against my better judgement, Lance persuaded me to let him take Blake to Spain on one final holiday. At first I was dead set against it. I said "no, the courts have made their ruling". But Lance was as persuasive as he had always been and convinced me that Blake would be amongst friends whom he knew.

'It's a holiday, Georgette, that's all!'

'I know, Lance, but ..'

'It's just with some friends, Blake knows them all.'

'I don't know ..'

'He's my son, for God's sake! I won't let anything happen to him.'

I don't know why I agreed. Maybe I'd forgotten how Lance could behave. Maybe I had something else on my mind. Maybe I let Lance persuade me, like I let him persuade me to marry him. Maybe the moon was blue or the sun was black or there were seven Mondays in the month. I don't know! Don't ask me! I only know I let him go. How could I have let him go? It's like, how could I have married Lance – how could I have been such a fool? It's the same kind of thing. It's so easy to be such a fool, when you don't know. I didn't know, and it's easy to be wise now, after the event – after so many events. So I let him go and that decision will haunt me forever!

He was seven years old.

'Ring me every day, darling. Mummy will blow you kisses at ten o'clock every night.'

But he didn't ring – wasn't allowed to ring. When I rang him, I either couldn't get through, or I was told he was in bed, sleeping. I convinced myself that he was having a good time and loads of fun and he was probably too tired to ring. I knew that wasn't the truth, but I convinced myself it was. To think anything else would have been unbearable.

Blake came home after a week and I was so thrilled to have him back. How I had missed him! We spoke about the holiday, and it was as if a coldness had come into the room somehow, from somewhere. It disturbed me and made me shiver. I kissed Blake and hugged him and told him over and over how much I'd missed him. But there was a sadness in his eyes. I told myself it was my imagination. I told myself maybe he missed the fun he was having in Spain and needed some time to adjust to being back in boring old England. Blake smiled and laughed, but the sadness remained. I tried to ignore it, not to think about it – because to think about it was to invite the unthinkable.

Finally, I asked.

'Did anything happen in Spain, Blake?'

'What do you mean, mummy?'

'I don't know .. anything?'

'I don't know what you mean, mummy. Lots of things happened.'

'Any bad things?

Something bad had happened, I was sure of it. Something terrible had happened. But I was convinced he'd blocked it out of his memory. He couldn't remember the bad thing, the terrible thing. Only the sadness.

I didn't ask him again. What do you say? Where do you begin? How can you ask a question, when you don't really want to hear the answer? So we let it lie, Blake and I. But the demon would come back to haunt us – nineteen years later.

Lance Fielder never saw Blake again, and I was happy to have him out of our lives at last. I spoke to him once more, many years later, when Blake was in Pentonville. By that time, there was nothing left of whatever small relationship there may have been between Blake and his natural father. Blake never doubted that I did the right thing in leaving Lance – he knew it was because of my love for him.

It was while Blake was there, in Pentonville, that we heard about the accident. Lance had fallen while out cycling and was completely paralysed from the neck down. We looked at each other, Blake and I, when we heard the news. We didn't speak, we didn't laugh, we didn't cry. We just looked at each other.

CHAPTER 3
EARLY LIFE – LONDON

We took a cab from King's Cross to Roach Road E3, where Alex lived. Alex Foden was Amy's hairdresser. I'd met him before and, despite the fact that he was rumoured to be a heavy drug-user, I liked him and I knew that he liked Blake, despite all the vindictiveness in the newspapers and magazines. It was late, dark. The city was hostile. Threatening. I imagined danger all around, on the long taxi ride to Stratford – up Caledonian Road past Pentonville Prison, which grinned at me as I passed and whispered "you'll be back". Then east through Islington and Hackney, into the Stratford Marsh area. People in the street looked across at us, as we passed them by – or so it seemed to me. Surreal, criminal faces peered into our cab when we stopped at traffic lights. They knew why we were here. They knew Blake had been arrested, the whole of London knew! It would be in all the papers. Then the name calling would begin again, they would use that word again and say it served him right – the junkie. The junkie loser! The junkie bastard!

We were in big trouble.

Amy was waiting for us outside the Amiga Buildings in Roach Road. We'd never been up there before and we weren't sure what to expect. Alex was with her. Amy ran to me and hugged me and I immediately asked her where Blake was being held.

'I don't know, momsie. They won't tell us.'

'We must find out!'

'They won't say.'

Amy and Alex took us round the back of the building, along an area of wooden decking, to Flat 65. Amy wanted Harry and Fred to go wait with a friend of hers called Tyler, who lived in one of the other flats. I didn't know why – maybe she anticipated the trouble that was to follow – and I didn't want my boys to leave my side, especially in this strange, dark place. But Tyler's flat was only a few feet away, along the decked area and Fred agreed to go there when he found out Tyler had XBox Elite. Harry didn't.

We saw Mitch Winehouse as soon as we entered Alex's flat. Giles had gone in first, followed by Amy and me, with Harry and Alex coming behind. Giles was still angry and went at Mitch, as soon as he saw him. There was already some animosity between the two of them and it spilled over.

'You've got some nerve being here, Mitch!'

'Say that again, and I'll sort you out, Giles.'

Giles said it again. I think Mitch threw the first punch, but I could be wrong. That's when all hell broke loose, with fists flying all over the place. I got involved and Amy got involved and Harry suddenly came from nowhere and started throwing punch after punch at Mitch. I'd never seen such anger in him before, in all his fifteen years. He was shouting at the top of his voice.

'You bastard, you set my brother up!'

Alex tried to stop Harry, but he couldn't. Mitch fell over a chair and Harry still kept throwing punches. Amy was screaming.

'Harry, please don't ..'

'Your dad set my brother up! It's my brother, and your dad set him up!'

'Stop it, Harry, please.'

I don't know why Harry shouted what he did. He knew nothing of the conspiracy, or of the warning I'd had from René, the supposed drug-dealer. I can only assume he'd gathered that Mitch hated Blake and wanted him away from Amy. He'd seen Mitch's protectiveness towards his daughter up close once, when he stayed with her and Blake. They went to a cinema and were just about to go inside, when Mitch suddenly turned up and began to shout at Amy, frog-marching her away like a naughty schoolgirl. Harry was surprised by the man's excessive behaviour – so, it was easy enough for him to make the assumption that, if Blake had been arrested, Mitch must have had something to do with it.

Then, just as quickly as it started, the fight stopped. The quietness of the aftermath was surreal. Unreal. We just stood looking at each other, as if we'd gone mad for a moment, as if we'd been temporarily insane, but now we'd come back to our senses. Nobody spoke, or moved, for a minute or two. Then Amy went unsteadily out of the room and that kind of broke the spell. We watched her go in a sort of surreal silence, then we started talking, tentatively at first, as if to change the subject of her erratic exit. Somebody poured drinks and we sat down. One minute we were all trying to kill each other and, the next minute, we were having a drink together and talking – not exactly as if it hadn't happened, but as if we wanted to pretend it hadn't happened.

That's when I noticed, for the first time, that there were other people in the room with us – maybe seven or eight, I'm not sure now. Dark, shadowy people. The room itself was dark and shadowy and the people were like phantoms – wraiths – sitting back in the gloom, in obscure corners. They hadn't interfered in the fight, just watched. They were smiling in a sinister kind of way – as if their faces were masks and the smiles had been painted on. They were not friendly smiles, neither were they unfriendly, they were more like grimaces. Deceptive – vague – eerie. Their eyes shone with a strange kind of tragic intensity. I felt I was close to something ephemeral – moribund, and it scared me. I had entered the world which I'd been trying to avoid for so long.

My son's world.

Blake was ten when I had Harry for Giles. We were living in Surrey, where Giles had his first teaching post. It was at Feltonfleet private school in Cobham and Blake was sent there, but he hated it and was desperate to leave. Again, I felt as if I was failing him – making him do something he didn't want to do. I didn't know it at the time, but Blake had begun to self-harm during the single year we spent in Surrey. He was careful to hide it from me and, as far as I know, it was a temporary phase which was only to return to him much later, when he went to Pentonville prison. But how could I have missed it? How? Was I too engrossed with my own life – with myself? How did I miss that? After everything that had happened with Lance – how could I have missed that?

Blake's relationship with Giles was strong enough at the time, at least I thought it was. He called Giles "daddy daydreams", a name that has survived the years, and he was really happy to have a younger brother, even thought the gap between them was quite large. But he was sad at the same time – the old sadness from before. It had stayed with him and was now being exacerbated by the circumstances of his life – even though I didn't realise it. I should have realised it, shouldn't I? I should have seen it – known it. But I suppose I was a different woman then and preoccupied with other things, things that preoccupy women with young families to bring up. So – I didn't!

As he got older, the bond between Blake and Giles grew weaker. This may have had something to do with Giles having been sent to a boarding school at the age of seven and having had no real relationship with his parents, having had problems relating in a family environment. Or it may have had something to do with Blake not being his natural son. Or something to do with Blake being a bit of a wild teenager – typical in a lot of ways – staying out late and using us as his personal taxi service – normal teenager behaviour, I suppose, to someone who'd had experience of normal teenager behaviour. But maybe not so easy to understand for someone who didn't.

Then, in 1994, I had Fred and Blake was unintentionally shoved a little bit further away from me. Looking back many years later, at the time I made my suicide pact, I knew exactly how Blake must have felt – alone in the midst of a family. Even so, there were no real signs of drugs or self-harming and the sadness of Surrey seemed to have been left behind – even if it was still there, lurking in the background. We moved to Bourne, in Lincolnshire, and Blake passed the entry test to Bourne Grammar School. He seemed to love that school, in total contrast to the private school in Surrey – he became very popular and he got on very well with all his teachers. They used to laugh and tell me, in a happy encouraging way, that the school was like a "social club" for Blake.

And, if Blake was happy, I was happy.

Until August 2001, when he decided to leave home and move to London. He was only seventeen. I didn't want him to go, not because I was worried about him becoming a drug-addict – that never even crossed my mind. I'd never noticed any of the signs of drug addiction during the years when he was growing up, so why should I be worried about something like that? Oh yes, I know – I know he experimented with a little cannabis, didn't every teenager?

'Everybody does a little cannabis, mum'

And he was right – even Bill Clinton when he was young – even Tony Blair. It was a harmless drug, a recreational drug, far less dangerous than alcohol. I wasn't worried, he was always in control of it. He was always lucid, never wasted. And there were never any hard drugs in the house. No Class A stuff.

No, it broke my heart when he told me he was going to London, because I believed he was happy at home and, if he was leaving home, then it must be because he wasn't happy there. He wasn't happy and I didn't know about it. What did that say about me as a mother? Blake just laughed it off and said he and his friend Paul had been thinking about it for some time and it would be great fun – a gas. I'd only met Paul once and he looked really ill at the time, sniffing and sweating – I didn't like the look of him at all. But Blake said he only had a cold and, stupidly I suppose, I believed him.

'I need to be out on my own, mum.'

'Why?'

'You can understand, mum .. you understand.'

But I didn't understand. We'd been together for so long – we'd been so close. My heart was filled with the old aching, as I watched him pack. I wanted to plead with him, to beg him not to go. But he was so excited, so full of expectation. How could I spoil it for him? Giles was blasé about it.

'He'll be back in a couple of weeks, once he gets it out of his system.'

'Will he, Giles?'

'Of course he will. He'll miss the comforts of home, don't you worry.'

But I did worry. I was dying inside. It was so difficult to let him go, yet I knew I had to do it. It was the right thing, I had to do the right thing. If I stopped him now, he'd only resent me for doing it, probably for the rest of his life. And maybe Giles was right, maybe he'd be back in a couple of weeks.

Blake found a flat in Acton with his friend Paul and he didn't come back in a couple of weeks. By Christmas he was working in hairdressing and he'd met a lovely girl called Jenny. He bought her a ring and they came home to visit for two weeks. He looked good and everything seemed to be going well. I relaxed.

I took on as many hairdressing clients in London as I could and, over the next couple of years, Blake and I availed of every opportunity to be together. I'd book into a hotel and we'd meet up for lunch or for a drink or for dinner somewhere – I'd use any excuse I could think of. It was wonderful to be with him on my own, like in the old days. We had such fun, sometimes being naughty and overspending on the hospitality bar. But that was us, always pushing boundaries. Maybe there were times when he was a little edgy – a little anxious. But, isn't everybody – at times? I never once thought it could be anything to do with drugs. I never saw any evidence of hard drugs and, if sometimes he seemed a little lost, I thought maybe it was because I was a little lost myself.

I've always been a very possessive mother and jealous of my son's company – I admit that. Blake and I had a very strong relationship, there was a stronger than average bond between us. We were two-of-a-kind, we thought the same thoughts, felt the same feelings, were happy together, sad together – it was a strange, obsessive kind of love. It was, and still is, a very intense kind of love. It was difficult for people around us to understand. They didn't understand and I don't blame them for not understanding. But I made no apologies for it then and I make non now. It was what it was, and it is what it will always be – even if I know I have to let it go.

Sadly, Blake's relationship with Jenny didn't last. But he still seemed happy and content. He always kept in touch and visited from time to time, sometimes bringing girlfriends with him. He met a young lady called Christie, who was very nice. She was loud and bubbly and confident and great with Harry and Fred. They dated for quite a while and seemed to go everywhere together, even to Thailand on holiday once. I'm not sure why that relationship ended, but it did, and Blake then started dating a girl called Chloe. She was so beautiful and Blake brought her home to meet us. It was 2003.

Chloe was a designer, who created clothes for celebrities, and she took Blake into that world with her. She'd bring him along on jobs and introduce him to the people she was working for and he soon became bored with the relatively tame world of hairdressing. Blake started doing video clips and gradually got himself involved in the music business – he did some work with Lilly Allen and other pop stars and he said it was something he'd always wanted to be involved in.

I didn't mind, if he was happy –

He came home quite often back then – with Chloe, at Christmas and holidays, whenever he could. Blake adored his brothers and they loved him. He was such a boisterous character – Harry had a petrol scooter and the three of them would climb onto it and ride up and down the lane, shouting and laughing. He'd sit with the boys in their bedrooms and compete on computer games with them for hours. We'd go out for lunch and bowling and eat too much and laugh at everything and everybody – Blake said he liked the bowling shoes so much, he was thinking of keeping them and leaving his own – things like that – things that might not seem so funny to other people, but which were hilarious to us – at the time. He hated getting up in the mornings and the boys would come in and jump all over him, then they'd have a play-fight. Giles would cook breakfast and we'd spend hours just chatting about nothing in particular.

He was such a messy, untidy devil when he was home and he'd unplug the hoover when I was busy cleaning and smile at me.

'A house is for living in, mum.'

I'd plump up the cushions and he'd jump on them and flatten them again.

'A home is a home, mum.'

That's how he was. He was spontaneous and scatterbrained and always full of fun. Giles and he seemed to gel again, now he was living away from home – he'd wait for Giles to roll up some cigarettes, then he'd creep over and steal them.

'We'll smoke all Daydreams' fags, mum, and drink some red wine.'

It was a standing joke and we all laughed about it. He had such a brilliant sense of humour, if you were in tune with him, and he was always able to make me smile.

'Smile, mum. You're beautiful when you smile.'

He was never afraid to express his feelings and he didn't care who heard him.

'I love you, mum.'

That was Blake, full of love and affection.

Back then.

When it was time for him to go back to London, we'd give him as much money as we could afford. My mother would buy him underwear, forgetting he was growing up and buying the wrong size. Blake would put them on his head and chase the boys about the house and scream.

'I'm going to kiss you to death!'

They would run like mad, laughing and screaming with delight.

Once, we gave him a TV to bring back with him and I giggled at the thought of him making his way through London carrying a television set. But he was such great fun and he looked good and seemed happy. There were no signs of drugs whatsoever. The boys were always sad when he had to leave to go back to London and the house always seemed so quiet without him. I always carried a photo of Blake's graduation dance in my purse – he looked so handsome. He would ask me sometimes.

'Is it still in your purse, mum?'

It always was. And still is.

Then, some time later, in 2005, Blake and I arranged to meet for dinner in Covent Garden. Chloe came along with Blake and, as soon as I saw him, I knew something was wrong. I'd been with a client and I was late and he was angry – uncharacteristically angry. He was speaking in a way I'd never heard him speak before – using an angry voice he'd never used before. At first he wasn't making sense. I was tired and stressed myself and I thought it might be me, maybe I was picking up the wrong signals, so I listened more carefully to what he was saying. He said he left home because he never felt he belonged. He blamed Giles – and me. He said he felt alienated.

'Why didn't you tell me, Blake?'

'Why didn't you listen, mum?'

'You didn't tell me.'

'I tried to tell you!'

I couldn't understand why he was saying these things – these horrible, nasty things. I was angry myself, listening to this, so I stormed out of the restaurant and went back to my hotel and cried. You have to understand, my love for Blake was unconditional – it didn't matter what he did, I still loved him. I wanted him to have a great future – a beautiful life. If I failed him, it was never intentional. If I didn't hear what he was saying to me, it was because I was too close to understand the words. If I had been a little more distant. If I didn't love him so much. If I'd been a better mother. If, if, if, if, if –

Blake rang me at the hotel – he apologised.

'I'm sorry, mum. I'm sorry.'

'It's alright, my darling. I'm sorry too.'

Blake and I had never fallen out before. We had never hurt each other before – or so I believed. Something had changed him, something had made him speak to me like that. For the first time, I asked myself the question – could my son be taking some kind of drugs? For the first time, I gave myself the right answer to that question. And it was the first time I realised that, perhaps, something was going wrong with Blake – something, for which I might only have myself to blame.

But the subliminal conviction didn't last for very long. I told myself that, if he was taking drugs, it was just recreational – occasional – he was mixing with people who lived that kind of lifestyle. Some of it was bound to rub off, but there was no real problem. How could there be?

A few weeks later, Blake telephoned me at home. He was a little upset and sounded depressed. He said he and Chloe had broken up and it was all his fault. He said he'd met another girl, while he was working in a bar in London, helping out a friend.

Her name was Amy Winehouse.

CHAPTER 4
AMY – ADDICTION

Amy and I went to check on Fred. Amy was laughing in an odd kind of way about the fight. It was as if she wasn't quite aware of why I was there, as if she'd forgotten about the telephone call she made to me.

'Blake will piss himself when I tell him.'

I didn't see the funny side – at least not then. Fred was fine and we walked back together to Alex's flat.

'Blake had a bad feeling all day, momsie .. he felt something was going to happen to him.'

'Well it did, Amy! Blake's in a police cell!'

'We took out eight grand .. you know, to keep Kelly going until ..'

She stopped. Maybe she realised she shouldn't be telling me this. Maybe she'd been briefed not to say anything more to me. She and Blake had said too much to me already about the plan to pay James King off.

The strange people were still in the flat when we got back – still looking strange. I wanted to find out exactly what had happened – even though I already had a fair idea.

'Does anyone know where he is?'

Mitch took over – began to play God, in that way of his, what seemed to me at the time a domineering way, a condescending way, a patronising way, a bullying way. But he was still a little wary of Harry, so his voice was appeasing .

'Blake will be out on bail in a few days, Georgette.'

'But where are they holding him?'

'We don't know.'

I thought he was lying. I believed he knew alright – that he was probably the only one who knew, apart from his friend at the Daily Mirror.

'What happened?'

'Our sailor's strong. He'll be OK.'

'Will he, Amy? You're as much involved in this as Blake.'

Mitch's face blanched at this remark, but he held his temper – just.

We tried to go over the events of yesterday evening, but it was difficult to pin down what had happened. Amy kept slipping off to the bedroom every few minutes and, even though we all had a fair idea why, we said nothing – we just watched, including her father, as she wasted herself.

'What happened, Amy?'

'Blake is strong. He'll be OK.'

'I know he's strong, but we can't let him stand alone.'

Mitch tried to say something else non-committal, I'm not sure what, but I was getting more and more stressed as the minutes ticked by. Time was passing and nobody seemed to care that Blake was passing that same time in a small, bare police cell. God knows what they were doing to him, saying to him, accusing him of.

'Listen Amy, if you think I'm saying nothing, think again. You told me on the phone about the money, I offered to deliver it myself ..'

'Stop it, momsie, you're worried .. we all are. Blake is strong.'

'You stop it, Amy!'

'Blake is strong, momsie ..'

That's all she said, over and over. Mitch jumped in quickly.

'Say nothing, Georgette! Do you hear me?'

'Listen Mitch, Amy's just as much involved in the payoff as Blake. I knew about it and, if I knew about it, so did you!'

Mitch kept shaking his head and trying to change the subject. He kept saying that Blake had hurt the King boy very badly and that's what all this trouble was about.

'I knew nothing, Georgette. Nobody said anything to me. This is all about King, Blake smashed his face in. He almost took his eye out.'

'I know what he did, Mitch!'

'How could you have said it was an accident?'

'I didn't say that! I said Blake's not a violent boy .. it must have got out of hand.'

I already knew what Blake had done. He told me himself and he was ashamed of it. He was so sorry, he even offered to pay medical expenses for James King's mother, who was very ill. I didn't need to hear it all again from Mitch. I was getting stressed out – ready to scream. I didn't want to hear any more crap either about Blake being a strong boy, or about the GBH charge. And, anyway, that wasn't why he'd been arrested, was it? He'd been arrested for conspiracy. How did the police find out about the conspiracy, that's what I wanted to know. I knew Mitch must have heard something – he and I were the only two who could know, apart from those directly involved – and I must have insinuated that he'd grassed. That made Mitch very angry again. He jumped to his feet, looking round at the strange people.

'For God's sake, Georgette .. never repeat what you just said, to anybody! If you do, you'll make things worse!'

'Worse for who, Mitch? Amy? You? Me?'

'I had nothing to do with this!'

'You're a liar .. and a Judas! And one day I'll prove it. My son's in deep shit, Mitch. I'm going to the police tomorrow. I'll make a statement. I'm not going to allow Blake to take the blame on his own.'

'Listen, Georgette, and listen very carefully .. Blake will get bail in a few days. If you make a statement, he'll never forgive you. Do you understand? Just leave it, he might not even be charged.'

I turned to Amy for help.

'Look at your father, Amy. He's not even shocked that you and I are both involved in the conspiracy. He hasn't asked any questions, does that not seem odd? We're both as guilty as Blake and your dad doesn't seem to care. Why did he take you out for dinner yesterday? How did the police know Blake was here? Do you understand what I'm saying, Amy?'

'Yes momsie .. you love Blake and you're feeling hurt.'

'Listen Amy, why did the police come here?'

'I was here.'

'Why didn't you go home?'

'I don't know.'

But I did!

That's the trouble with Amy. She's so trusting of a lot of people, even if she sometimes doesn't quite know why – people who don't have her best interests at heart. And, contrary to popular opinion, Blake wasn't one of those people. In fact, he was the only one she could trust, despite what the papers were saying.

During the couple of years leading up to their marriage, it seemed to me that Blake and Amy had very much an on-off relationship. I know Blake was dating Chloe as well and maybe some other girls too. So, Amy was just "Amy" to me, one of the young ladies he knew in London and mentioned to me from time to time on the phone. I didn't really know anything about her and, for a while, I even thought she was Lilly Allen or some other young, female pop-star. Blake would laugh at me when I said silly things like that.

'Get with it, mum.'

'How am I supposed to know, Blake?'

'Don't worry, I'll keep you in touch.'

Even then, Amy was showing signs of being a very unpredictable young lady. Her drinking was being publicised and she was failing to turn up for gigs, she was even accused of being violent towards some of her own fans. Blake was also an unpredictable young person and their coming together fuelled that unpredictability in both of them. But neither of them had any criminal history back then, either for violence or drugs, and none of their friends were running to the press with stories to make money. I know they won't agree, but it was, like, both of them were in the wrong place at the wrong time – that day they met. They fell in love, and it was a love that almost destroyed them both. But, as a mother, I have absolutely no say in who my son falls in love with, no more than Amy's parents have any say in who their daughter falls in love with.

Isn't that so?

I'd read about celebrity lifestyles and I suppose the thought of drugs was always somewhere at the back of my mind – but it wasn't a major concern. Blake was a bit of a wild boy and certainly no angel, but I never once thought he might get involved with hard drugs, never mind become addicted to them. I mean, I never saw needle marks on his arms – so how could he be on heroin? I didn't know that addicts injected their ankles and feet and even their private parts, as well as their arms – or that heroin could be snorted and smoked and squirted up the nostril with a syringe. How could I know such things back then? I was an ordinary hairdresser, living in an ordinary little village in Lincolnshire – I was married to an ordinary schoolteacher and I led, for the most part, a very ordinary life.

Nor did I know anything about cocaine or crack or whatever else they called the stuff. I didn't know anything about the signs of these drugs – the signs to look out for – like depression and insomnia and self-harming and suicidal behaviour with heroin, and confusion and anxiety and nosebleeds with cocaine. I didn't know what to look out for and, even if I did, I didn't know I ought to be looking out for anything. If I had, I might have taken more notice, I might have been more aware. But Blake seemed to be having fun with Amy – they would go to clubs together, or to the cinema, or to the park and take food and drink with them for picnics and they'd have a few glasses of wine and get silly together. You know, the kind of harmless things young people do when they're in the early stages of a relationship and infatuated with each other.

But something else was beginning to manifest itself. The closer Blake and Amy grew together, the more protective Mitch Winehouse seemed to become. He'd turned into a very possessive father when Amy began to make a name for herself in the music business. He would say that Blake was getting "too close" to Amy for his liking. Maybe he thought Blake was only with her because she was starting to be recognised as the great singer she is and he was using her to make connections in the pop-star world, or as a meal-ticket, or as a useful way of furthering his own career. But Mitch couldn't have been more mistaken. The problem was, he'd never seen Amy so much in love before and he didn't understand that kind of affection. He'd never given her love like that and now his perception of someone who did was biased and corrupted by his own rivalry for his daughter's affection.

Blake came back home for a few days after he finally broke up for good with Chloe and I had a chance to be with him and to see how he really was. Despite my earlier self-recrimination for what happened with Lance Fielder and with Blake's sudden departure for London and his uncharacteristic behaviour in the Covent Garden restaurant, things seemed to be going well for him again and I told myself that everyone has setbacks. Every family has its problems to deal with and my family was no different. I told myself that I had probably overreacted to Covent Garden – that I had maybe mis-read the signs – that I wasn't a bad mother and I shouldn't blame myself for having a normal family, with normal family problems. I reproached myself for playing the martyr, for being a bit melodramatic, for overcooking the cake of self-guilt.

Blake was sad about the breakup with Chloe, not because they'd split up, but because he'd been seeing both her and Amy at the same time and he felt guilty about that. Apart from a little melancholy on that count, he looked good and I was happy to have him home, even if it was only for a few days. He and Amy were constantly telephoning and texting each other while he was with me and they seemed to be so much in love. I still didn't really know who Amy Winehouse was, I'd never heard the name until that day when Blake phoned and said he'd met her. She wasn't as famous then, or as infamous, as she became after she married Blake. But, at that time, he seemed happy and full of life and I didn't really care what her name was, as long as she and Blake were good together.

I know now that they were both experimenting to some extent with hard drugs before they met each other and I know the usage of those hard drugs accelerated after they got married. I also know that not everyone who experiments with drugs ends up addicted to them. The problems Blake had in his early young life may have contributed to his tendency towards addiction. The scars were there, on his psyche – lying dormant, waiting to be triggered. I accept my share of the blame for those scars. The scars on Amy's psyche, that made her just as susceptible to addiction as Blake, were already there, before she met him. It's not my intention to apportion blame for those scars. That's something which has to be addressed by Amy and her own family.

So, life went on. Blake in London with Amy and the people who were gathering round her. Giles and I with the boys. I don't think any of us knew what was round the corner. We just went on with our lives like anyone else. I was busy with my business and with bringing up Harry and Fred. Giles was busy with his teaching and also playing his part in bringing up our two sons. Hurricane Katrina hit New Orleans, we were all worried about bird flu, the war raged on in Iraq, Roger Federer won Wimbledon, we had a heat-wave in the summer. Deciding to kill myself and to take my three sons with me was the very furthest thing from my mind.

Even when Blake called me one night, very upset. I asked him what was wrong and, for a while, he wouldn't say. But he sounded very sad and I kept on pressing him. Finally, he came out with what was on his mind.

'It's Amy, mum .. she gets a bit violent when she can't have her own way.'

'What do you meant, violent?'

'Just .. violent, mum.'

I could hear Amy shouting in the background. There were other people there as well. I could hear lots of voices.

'See what I mean, mum? I love her, but I don't like the violence.'

'Blake .. come home! I'll come get you .. bring you home.'

'I miss you so much sometimes, mum.'

Amy was still shouting in the background. I could hear her coming closer to the phone.

'You always do it, Blake, don't you ..'

'What does she mean, darling?'

'It's because I called you, mum. It'll be OK, don't worry."

As I've already said, Blake and I had a unique relationship, stronger than the average mother-son bond. It wasn't an Oedipus Rex scenario or anything like that, but it was special. It scared me at times, it went so deep. Perhaps it came from somewhere in the past, not the immediate past of our current lives, but a more remote past, in another time – another incarnation. I just know there was nothing I wouldn't have done for him. Nothing!

I tried to keep him on the phone, to keep him away from the violence, whatever that violence might be. I wanted to run down to London and hug him and bring him home, but I knew he didn't want me to do that. That wasn't why he called. He called because he was lonely, even though there were lots of people around him. It wouldn't be very long before I knew that feeling myself – intimately.

'I love you, mum.'

Then he hung up the phone. I didn't sleep much that night. Giles said not to worry, Blake wouldn't put up with that kind of thing for very long. Giles was always pragmatic. He told me not to get involved, I'd only make matters worse.

'They'll be friends tomorrow, Georgette. You'll see.'

And he was right. Mothers just can't go around getting involved in their son's lives every time there's a little bit of trouble. Can they?

Amy Winehouse brought out her new album, "Back to Black" soon after. It was a wonderful jazz-soul album, which received universal critical acclaim and made her an international star. Amy dedicated the record to Blake and said she could never have made it without him. That's when the trouble really began.

Towards the end of this time, Blake was with a friend of his called Michael Brown. There was a girl who was dating Brown and then she began dating a man called James King. It was just one of those things – one of those circumstantial things that happen. A random meeting. In a pub – outside a pub, I can't remember and it doesn't matter. What matters is the circumstance – the occurrence – the happening – the random circumstantial meeting. Brown and King just happened to meet up with each other one night – just happened to be in the same pub – just happened to pass each other – just happened to see each other. A fight started.

Blake was with Brown.

Shit can happen as easily as that.

CHAPTER 5
MARRIAGE – THE MEDIA

It seemed obvious to me, at least, that Mitch had planned this in some way. He took Amy to dinner to get her out of the way. But the plan backfired a bit, because Blake didn't stay at the flat in Camden like he was supposed to – he wasn't there when the police came and broke the door down.

Amy was looking at me, watching me. I could see she felt sorry for me and I felt sorry for her, but she just smiled in that enigmatic way of hers and said that I shouldn't worry, because Blake was strong. I reminded her about my phone call to her and Blake, the night René Butler came to see me – about the diagram he drew for me, the symbol with the words "bitch" and "snitch" and "mitch" (copy available). As Blake wasn't at Camden, where he was supposed to be, somebody had to have told the police where to find him. That somebody was the "snitch". It was obvious who "mitch" was and René the drug-dealer had already identified the "bitch" for me.

'I think your father was involved in having my son, and your husband, arrested, Amy.'

Amy looked at Mitch. I don't know if she could remember my phone call about the warning – there was a puzzled look on her face. But she did become angry with her father for a brief moment and, to her credit, she flashed an accusing look his way.

'Dad ..?'

But it was only for a brief moment – then the moment went. I don't think she was in any state to really understand what was happening. Mitch was furious.

'That's nonsense! You're mad, Georgette!'

'What about your friends .. the bitch and the snitch? Look your daughter straight in the eye, tell her you weren't involved. Go on! You can't, can you?'

My heart was racing, I could see all the blank, mindless faces around me. Alex tried to calm me. I wanted to scream and hit out at Mitch, his eyes looked full of guilt – or maybe it was hatred for me. Either way, I hated him in return. My anger was rubbing off on Harry, he was getting agitated again. He'd been listening to what I was saying and he knew something was rotten here. I could hear him growling under his breath.

'He's my brother, and I love him.'

Poor Harry, I could see his sadness, feel his anger. Mitch looked a little cowed and mumbled something indecipherable, but affirmative, about a couple of friends of his who might be saying something to the papers.

'But nobody would ever do anything to hurt Blake, Georgette.'

'Why, Mitch? Was it money .. or jealousy?'

'I'm sorry, Georgette.'

'One day the truth will come out and, when it does, how will you expect Amy to forgive you. I know I never will.'

'Why would I hurt Blake, Georgette?'

'Because you hate him!'

'I don't hate him.'

'Everyone knows you do!'

Mitch didn't answer. I looked him straight in the eye – to me, right then, it was like looking into the cold eyes of a snake. He couldn't hold my gaze and he turned away from me. Amy put her arm round my shoulders.

'My dad loves Blake, momsie ..'

'That's bollocks, Amy!'

I didn't want to swear, but I couldn't control myself. Mitch tried to protest his innocence again, but I wasn't listening anymore. Amy was being even more erratic by now and saying over and over how much she loved Blake and how he would be OK and how he would be home in a few days. The strange people were getting stranger by the minute and I knew it was hopeless. I wanted to cry and scream at the same time – even laugh out loud at the sheer surreality of it all. I was surrounded by people with no souls, with no hearts – their only desire was to either be bystanders at the event, or to protect themselves, they certainly didn't care about my Blake. It was very late and I realised there was nothing more to be done here. I'd find out where Blake was tomorrow.

We collected Fred and Mitch insisted on driving us to our hotel. I wanted to take a taxi, but he wouldn't allow it. He was conciliatory again – appeasing again, not wanting to antagonise me and force my hand.

'We shouldn't be fighting like this, Georgette.'

'Blake's not going to be left out in the cold, Mitch.'

He thought for a moment, trying to work out how to settle the situation – how to make me see his version of reason.

'Listen .. I found out tonight who's been supplying Amy with the drugs.'

'Who?'

'Julianne.'

At first I didn't know why he was telling me this, Julianne (not real name) known for a while – I believed she was a good friend of the Winehouse family and she had a beautiful eleven-year-old daughter. Mitch said she'd been at Roach Road earlier and she left not long before we arrived – he said we may even have passed her on our way in. It shocked me in a way, that he was admitting this, until I realised he wasn't telling me to make me feel better, he was making a point.

'I don't know what to do about it.'

'You have to tell the police, Mitch.'

'What about her daughter, she could be taken into care. I'd never forgive myself.'

'What about your own daughter?'

'And your sons .. Georgette?'

I knew then he wasn't going to do anything about it. Mitch had mentioned Julianne's daughter for a reason. I was convinced Blake had been set up, my son had been led like a lamb to slaughter. And now Mitch was forcing me to face my own predicament – because of my knowledge and involvement. If I went to the police with what I knew, it was a foregone conclusion I'd be arrested and probably prosecuted. What would happen to my other sons then? What would happen to Fred and Harry? If I did nothing, Blake would take the punishment for all of us – Amy, me, Mitch and God knows who else. Fred slipped his hand into mine – he looked at me and smiled.

'Please don't be unhappy mummy.'

I knew then that Mitch would win. He would have his way. Blake would be sacrificed to save the rest of us.

Giles and I settled the boys into their beds at the hotel. It had all been so traumatic and they were tired. Giles wanted to know what had happened, what was all that about with Mitch. I told him it was nothing – it was just Mitch being Mitch. Giles was exhausted and didn't really want to talk about it any more, so he went to bed. I poured a drink and looked out through the window, at the dark London night. The events of the evening flashed through my mind. Everything had been fine just a few short hours earlier – everything had been normal – usual, you know, the usual things that happen to usual people – normal people. Now my son was in a cell, he was probably disorientated and confused. I didn't even know where he was and I was powerless to help him. I prayed to God to let him know that I was near him, to let him feel my love, to protect him.

'Please Lord!'

Even then, I was pretending I didn't realise my prayers were imposters – because I had buried my head in the sand for so long about the drugs and I knew about the conspiracy and I had ignored the warning that was given to me and I was, therefore, one of the people who had helped put him where he was.

'Never be a hypocrite.'

That was the advice my father used to give me when I was young. I've always tried to heed that advice. I've tried to be straight in my dealings with people and I've tried to be as honest as possible with myself. At least, that was the opinion I had of myself at one time in the past.

Long before I made the suicide pact.

After the fight in the pub with King, Blake and Amy went away to Canada. He telephoned me from there and told me he wanted to marry Amy and would we come over for the wedding.

'Of course! Of course!'

Giles was involved with SATS exams at school, but the boys and I would come.

'I'll let you know the date and sort out the tickets, mum.'

He was so excited. A few days later, Blake telephoned again. They were in America.

'We're not in Canada any more, mum. We're in the States.'

We laughed together and I said it was a good job we didn't fly over after the first phone call, we'd be in two different countries now. He couldn't stop telling me how wonderful Amy was and how very much he loved her. I asked if he still wanted us to come over, he said he'd let me know.

Blake called again a few days later.

'I'm the happiest man alive, mum. Would you like to speak to my wife?'

'Your wife?'

'Amy is my wife now. And I'm the happiest man in the world.'

Blake and Amy got married on 18th May 2007. Amy came on the phone.

'Hello, momsie, how are you?'

We giggled a bit at the name she called me and I offered her my congratulations. She said thank you – momsie. And giggled again.

'Your son is so gorgeous. I love him to death.'

Blake brought Amy to meet us when they got back, a few weeks later, and I could see for myself how much they meant to each other.

'You'll love her as much as I do, mum.'

I did. She was so beautiful, so small – a "titch", like me. If Blake left the room, Amy followed and if Amy went, Blake wasn't far behind her – maybe I should have asked what they were leaving the room for, but I didn't, Blake was happy and you know how it was. If Blake was happy –

They spent the night with us and we all had a great time, laughing and talking, with Amy and I getting to know each other. Next day I took her to see the salon, because she said she'd always wanted to be a hairdresser – she had her big trademark beehive by then and I loved it, it was so unique. Such big hair for such a little lady. Amy did her nails at the salon and then we went for lunch. And I found myself liking this girl – and I believe she liked me. She was such a loving person. Blake asked me to give her a piece of my jewellery, I don't know why, maybe to form some bond between us and I had no problem with that. I gave her a silver bracelet which my family had given to me many years before. It was full of little charms celebrating births, marriages, special days and it was, if you like, a kind of bijou-record of my life. Amy loved that charm bracelet and she wore it often on tour. She was also very taken with my grandmother's ring, which I'd given to Blake, and which he gave to her as a present as soon as he found out she liked it.

I think she still has that jewellery. I hope she has.

We didn't meet Amy's father until some time after the wedding. I have never met her mother, her natural mother, face to face. Amy soon realised that, whenever I visited her and Blake, Mitch Winehouse would somehow find out and telephone the flat . Then, shortly after, he would turn up and I never seemed to be able to have time with them alone. Mitch would just roll up and take over. Amy once asked me if I wanted her to tell him to leave – how could I ask her to do that? He was her father. On a couple of occasions, Blake reminded her that I had travelled a long way to see them.

'Can't your father stay away just once?'

Amy always said her father was jealous of our close relationship. He was particularly critical of my relationship with Blake.

'She never sees any wrong in him, Amy!'

She didn't get on all that well with her own mother, that's why she called me "momsie". Her father hated it.

'She's not your mother, Amy!'

But Amy didn't care. She had such a sparkling sense of humour and she'd often ring Salon 54 and pretend to be someone else, or encourage me to play pranks on the media. Once, when the press were outside the salon, I rang a number Amy gave me and told them in an assumed accent that Georgette Civil had collapsed and was in hospital. They all immediately disappeared – where they went, I don't know, probably checking out every hospital in the area to see if I'd fell down from a drug overdose or some other such rubbish. While, all the time, I was in the salon, having my hair coloured. Next day, the tabloids printed some cock-and-bull story and Amy and I had a terrific laugh about it. That's how it was between us – we had a solid relationship and we loved to laugh together and talk about Blake and just be friends – real friends!

She and Blake often spoke about buying a hairdressing salon in London, with three stories – the top story for Blake, to do his music, the second floor for her, to chill out when she felt like it, and the ground floor for me, to do my thing with the hair.

'I love you, momsie."

'I love you too, Amy.'

It was a wonderful time then, before all the recriminations. They were so good together and seemed so innocent. I know people won't believe that, but they were! I saw it! Him with his hat, cocked on the side of his head and his Blues Brothers suit and her with her hairstyle and seductive smile. They had so much love for each other and there was nothing nasty or ugly about it that I could see.

I remember meeting them in the many hotels they frequented. I would take Harry and Fed with me sometimes and we'd have fun together, ordering everything on the menu and just having a good time. Amy was amazing with the boys and they were great with her. I even allowed my younger sons to stay with them on their own at times and to go on tour with them, when they weren't at school. Why shouldn't I? They went to the MTV awards in Munich and to Milan and Paris and Fred was introduced to Razorlight and performed for a TV programme there. The boys had such great fun together – Blake and Harry and Fred. But "great fun" doesn't sell newspapers, so nobody saw this period – this golden time – except me.

Why would I allow my two young sons to go off to places with a pair of "junkies"? I wouldn't! But I saw no sign of hard drugs back then. I saw no sign of addiction in either Blake or Amy. They didn't have dark rings round their eyes, they didn't slur their words, they didn't keep falling over, they didn't shout and scream at each other, they didn't look like the living dead. They were just two larger-than-life people, having the time of their lives – at least, that's what I thought. But then, I didn't know that people on hard drugs could look like larger-than-life people, having the time of their lives.

Soon, however, the media was reporting a very different picture – a picture of drugs and fighting and self-harming. They said Blake and

Amy were cutting each other and all kinds of other rubbish. There were pictures, but I refused to believe them and went down to London to see what was going on. Yes, there had been a bit of a scrap after a few drinks, but every couple has a scrap now and then, especially after a few drinks. But the media circus was in the mood for a culprit, a man to mark. Blake fitted the bill.

The truth of the matter is that Amy was taking drugs before she met Blake and Blake was taking drugs before he met Amy. So, how could one person be blamed? How could it all be Blake's fault? As far as I know, Amy's drug-taking accelerated in 2006, after her grandmother Cynthia died. She hadn't been with Blake for a great deal of time and her management team was already intimating that they were concerned about her. The media had to blame somebody and Blake was a convenient scapegoat – it was a great story "Good Girl, Bad Guy". It was manna from heaven for them. I'm not saying here that Blake was whiter than white. I know now there were drugs, even if I didn't admit it then. What I am saying is that I believe Amy would have become addicted with or without Blake – he was just a catalyst, a trigger maybe, for whatever was already inside her.

Blake hated how the media treated him. He often told Amy how he felt about it, but she seemed unconcerned and dismissed it all.

'It's just bollocks, Blake.'

That was one of her favourite retorts. He asked her to put the record straight and sometimes she would. But mostly the attention didn't bother her too much. There was one occasion, when Amy's manager, Raye, told Blake a report would be out in the papers, blaming him for some row or self-harming rubbish. He rang to warn me and I was furious. I made Giles ring Amy to complain – how could she allow Blake to take the blame for something like that? Hadn't he been blamed for enough already? She agreed, and put a stop to the report. But that was just one occasion. There were many, many others, when nobody intervened on my son's behalf – not even me.

By now the media pack was in full cry. They were killing Blake because, they said, he was killing Amy. Amy, to tell the truth, would always defend Blake to me when I tried to find out what was going on.

She would say he wasn't doing the kind of things they said he was, and neither was she. I always wanted to believe her, so I did.

'If that's the case, Amy, why don't you make a statement to the press, to help him?'

'Forget the media, momsie, they're nothing, just liars!'

But the lies kept coming, day in and day out. Both of them were starting to look a bit of a mess and Blake was blamed every time. Everywhere I went I could see the images and hear the words.

'Junkie! Junkie loser!'

I wanted to shout.

'He's not! He's Blake! My Blake, who I love!'

How could I win against the mass ranks of the media? One small woman against the frenzied, baying mob? I couldn't do it alone and I kept trying to get Amy to help.

'Please do something, Amy!'

'Forget them, momsie, they're idiots!'

'But they're hurting Blake .. and the boys at school .. me too, at the salon.'

'Trust me, momsie, nobody cares what they write.'

'I care, Amy! It's my son .. and your husband!'

But Amy just believed the media were idiots and nobody took any notice of them. They weren't blaming her, were they? The man she loved was taking all the crap. The press swarmed all over the place, like insects – outside our house, at my place of work, in the village –

'How d'you feel having a son who's a junkie?'

But I didn't believe I had a son who was a "junkie", or an "addict". As far as I was concerned, they just wanted a reaction, some more sensation to report – and sometimes I gave it to them. Who wouldn't?

There's not much doubt that I was kidding myself back then. I suppose I wanted to be blind to what was glaringly obvious? But I couldn't understand how two people who were so happy together and so loving and so full of fun could change so drastically? How could they become evil, when they were so good? Even now, I believe this change came about when other people became involved. I believe it was in some people's interest to encourage the deterioration of two young people who may have been experimenting with drugs, as many young people do, but who weren't, in their naiveté, interesting enough for the insatiable beast that is celebrity journalism!

So the trigger was pulled.

I try to look back now and criticise myself for not seeing. I look for the word I should have said, but there is no word. And, if there is no word, how can you say it? Maybe I was blind or maybe I was just as naive as Blake and Amy. To me, drug-addicts sat in doorways, or in filthy crack-houses, or public toilets – you know, the way I was told they live, the way I read they lived, in the darkest places on earth. Neither Blake nor Amy fitted that scenario, they didn't portray that image back then, before they got married. I used to ask myself if I was the only mother like that – who didn't see the signs – who refused to see the signs. If I was alone in the world.

Maybe I'm just a stupid, trusting, clueless woman, but I saw only love then. I saw no hatred, no vindictiveness, no ugliness – until the newspapers began to show it to the world. The stories started. The pictures appeared. I hardly knew Blake in the photographs, he looked like a stranger to me. Where did all this come from, so suddenly? I couldn't believe what I was reading. I couldn't believe what I was seeing. What had happened, in so short a period of time? What could possibly have happened?

And now it's all a matter of record, whether truth or lies – stuff that people read in the tabloids and magazines and then throw away – forget – are unconcerned about for very long. But, what if you can't throw it away? What if you can't get rid of it? What if you can't forget about it – can't let it go?

CHAPTER 6
MITCH – REHAB

Next day, which was Saturday, Mitch continued to convince me that Blake would be out on bail the following Monday, after he'd made an appearance in court.

'It's the weekend, Georgette, there's nothing we can do till Monday.'

'I want to see my son.'

'They won't let you.'

The thing is, Blake was already on bail for the GBH charge. So, of course, there was no way he would get bail again, and Mitch knew this. I had to get in contact with the solicitor who was handling the case, but both Mitch and Amy were reluctant to give me the phone number. I couldn't understand why that was, if it wasn't because someone was worried that I might say what I knew. In the end, Giles was forced to get angry with Mitch before we were given the details.

Kate Anderson was Blake's solicitor, and she told us he was being held at Stoke Newington police station in North London, but we would not be allowed to see him. She also told us that she believed Blake would be given bail on Monday, even though she probably suspected he wouldn't. So, we decided it was best to come home and wait for the long weekend to pass. I telephoned the police station at Stoke Newington, trying to speak to Blake, but they refused to allow it and just told me they would pass my message on – which I'm sure they didn't.

My mother and I went back down to London for the bail hearing on Monday 12th November. When we arrived at Snaresbrook courthouse, the place was crawling with press. We were met by Kate Anderson – it was the first time I'd met her and she took us into a back room to explain that Blake could get bail, because all the evidence wasn't yet available. We knew only that the police had some video evidence which involved Blake in the conspiracy. Amy's security people were there and we were told she was on her way. I saw Blake when I came into the court – he looked drained. He blew me a kiss and I mouthed "I love you" back to him. I tried to hard not to cry.

And, of course, Blake didn't get bail. He was remanded to Pentonville prison instead and another hearing was set for the 23rd November. Amy didn't turn up and neither did Mitch. It was all over so quickly. Blake looked gaunt and pale, the judge looked pompous and self-opinionated, the prosecution looked pleased and Blake's defence looked resigned – not really all that surprised. Blake was taken down and I'll never forget his face as he looked towards me – it was full of sadness, full of regret, full of loneliness. He wasn't coming home, and there was nothing I could do to make that happen.

Kate Anderson took us back to the room in the courthouse. She told us not to worry, because there wasn't enough evidence for a conviction. Everything would be OK. I believed her, even though she'd been wrong about the bail – I had to believe her. It was the only chink of light I had. She told me I could write a note for Blake, but he would have to give it back. I wrote –

"I love you so very much, my darling. Grandma
and I will stay in London until we can see you."

The note came back. He'd written on it –

"Mum, grandma, you both looked beautiful today.
Be brave. Love you very much.
Blakie"

I couldn't hold the tears back any longer.

Kate Anderson came back to our hotel in Kensington with us. She told us that Blake would need clothes and money in Pentonville. I had absolutely no idea how to do anything, and my mother knew even less. The solicitor gave us a few instructions and then left, and we found ourselves alone in a new and intimidating situation. We would have to find out what was what – and fast!

About ten o'clock that night, Mitch Winehouse telephoned me on my mobile. I put the phone on loudspeaker, so my mother could hear what he had to say. He again made it very clear that I must not repeat to anyone what I knew about the payoff conspiracy. He said Blake would be "safe" in prison, that he would be "looked after". Both mum and I took this as a threat, that Amy must not be implicated in any way, or that something bad might happen to Blake. We had to be very, very careful.

It took days to sort out a prison visit. I didn't understand how the whole ridiculous system worked. We had to actually go to Pentonville to book the visit, where we were told how much money he could have and how to make the payments. He could have clothes, but no deodorants, no aftershave and no razors. We were shunted around the place, from one area to another, given one set of rules after another, made to wait for one self-important jobsworth after another, to arrange this and that and the other. All I wanted was to see Blake – I was on the edge, almost frantic, desperate for a glimpse of my son. But he was locked away from me. We were eventually given a visiting order for Wednesday 14th November, at two o'clock – to see prisoner WA7614. It was all so officious, so cold, so heartless – without any humanity whatsoever.

I was still worried about Mitch's implied threat about Blake being "safe and looked after" in prison – as long as I behaved. I had a good relationship with a certain young reporter called Sadie and I rang her and told her everything, because I wanted a record, on file, of the whole sorry conspiracy episode – just in case anything happened to Blake or myself. I needed to tell someone, someone who would back me up if it came to it and confirm that I told her at the time it happened, not twelve months later. The time was important to me, it mattered. It meant that I didn't imagine it, nor did I embellish it over the months or years, nor was I influenced by what was written in the newspapers. I made her promise never to leak the story to the press.

To this day, she has kept her word.

If you can't keep your word, what can you keep?

I had promised Blake that we would never be separated again – back then, after the courts had stopped Lance Fielder from taking him away from me. But I didn't keep my word. I allowed Lance to take him away to Spain that last time, and now I was allowing something else to take him away from me – drugs. Of course, I didn't admit it. The reports in the media were becoming more and more lurid every day. Terrible reports, about both Blake and Amy. Amy was always so very reassuring to me.

'It's all bollocks, momsie! Never believe what you read.'

And I didn't believe it. I didn't, despite the fact that it was there every day, shouting at me from the pages. I should have realised the photographs didn't lie. I should have seen what I previously didn't want to see, Blake looking gaunt and strange, Amy looking equally and increasingly thin and wasted. These images were the images I had in my head about how drug-addicts should look – the dark rings, the erratic behaviour, the sinister rooms, the shadowy world of a lifestyle which was totally alien to me.

I suppose I went into denial. It's such a powerful thing, denial – a bit like addiction, really. How could my Blake and his lovely wife be addicts? Who were these people who were insinuating such things? Yes, I know, both Giles and I went on the radio at times, saying we believed there was a problem and we were all looking for a solution to that problem. But that was on the radio, for the benefit of the listeners who were reading the papers – I kept telling myself there was no real problem.

Mitch continued to try to convince me there was a problem, every time I spoke to him. And he was right. Perhaps I resented him for being right, perhaps I didn't want him to be right, I don't know. There was something about his self-righteousness that rubbed me up the wrong way. According to him, the problem was Blake's and, if Blake wasn't with Amy, she'd be OK. I couldn't agree with that, of course. Amy's problem wasn't Blake, but Mitch always insisted it was.

'Let's try and separate them, Georgette. Let's get them into separate rehabs.'

All the time, the same thing. If Blake wasn't around, if Blake wasn't this, if Blake wasn't that. So, maybe I denied the problem because I was denying Mitch's assertions? Who knows? It all sounds so ridiculous now, yes there is a problem, no there isn't – one minute I'd be thinking "yes" and the next minute I'd be thinking "no". Then something else would happen and I'd be back where I started. In the end, I didn't know what to think.

I'd been down to their flat in Camden and, at times, Amy did seem to be having highs and lows – sometimes a little hyperactive, then a little quiet. She seemed sometimes to be more withdrawn than she had been, than the old Amy who I knew and loved. Blake was always Blake, noisy and naughty, while Amy would be quiet, then five minutes later she'd be back laughing and chatting. The change in Amy was more obvious to me than the change in Blake. Perhaps that was because I didn't want to see the change in Blake. We would go to the pub for a drink, Amy would disappear somewhere and Blake would get cross with her. When that happened, she would catch my arm.

'Tell him not to be cross with me, momsie.'

And I would.

Blake and Amy were changing, but I still refused to believe it was drugs that was changing them. I still made excuses to myself. That's what mothers do, isn't it? Or just this mother? Things will be OK tomorrow. Tomorrow things will be back to normal. Neither Mitch nor Giles wanted me to leave the boys with them any more and we rowed over it. But I refused to give in – they were Blake's brothers! If I refused to allow Harry and Fred to stay with Blake and Amy, then I was endorsing all the lies that had been written about them – that was never going to happen!

Gradually, however, I was forced to admit there really was some kind of problem. What that problem was, I still wasn't prepared to come to terms with. I continued to see only two young people who were being controlled by the forces around them and who would eventually realise what was happening to them and come to their senses.

But then Amy was rushed to hospital with a suspected overdose and it was very serious. I first heard about it when Mitch Winehouse telephoned to arrange a meeting. At first I didn't believe what he was saying. He was up to his controlling self again. Blake and Amy might be doing a little drugs, but not to that extent? Surely? It was just the papers being paranoid. I'd seen them together – Amy was so loving and generous. So beautiful. And Blake was so full of life. But, that was the way they were before, not now. And, at the back of my mind I knew there was something wrong. So, Giles and I went along to the meeting at the Four Seasons Hotel in rural Hampshire.

Mitch met us.

'We need to sort out this problem, Georgette.'

'What problem, Mitch?'

'Blake's!'

I was about to tell him what I thought, but decided to wait. Blake arrived before Amy and sat with Giles and I. I was so glad, I needed to see him, to reassure myself. Then Amy arrived and immediately ran over and hugged us all. We sat together and laughed and chatted as if nothing was wrong.

'Why are we here, Blake?'

'I'll tell you later. Amy and I are so pleased you're here, mum. We feel safe.'

'You are safe, darling. Are you in trouble?'

'I'll tell you later.'

Blake and Amy went off to their room to get ready for dinner. They both looked well – a bit edgy, maybe, but happy. At dinner, Mitch elaborated on Amy's emergency stay in hospital, due to the drug overdose.

'Blake may have saved her life, but he gave her the drugs in the first place.'

I couldn't believe what Mitch had just said. I knew he was talking nonsense – wasn't he? We both knew who was supplying Amy with drugs, and it wasn't Blake. Angry words followed, from both sides, I can't remember them now, but they were accusing, derogatory, insinuating, uncomfortable words. Amy was all over the place, up and down to her room. Mitch watched her, shaking his head.

'That's the drugs, that's what it is!'

I took Blake outside.

'Yes, mum, Amy did go to hospital. I did save her life. I don't really know what happened. Mitch is trying to separate us, he threw me out of the hospital. He tried to hide her from me, but Amy stole a mobile and told me where she was.'

'That's crazy, Blake. Amy's your wife and you're her husband. Her father can't do that!'

'He hates me, mum.'

Amy joined us. She draped her arms around Blake and said how sorry she was about what Mitch had done at the hospital.

'I don't know what his problem is, momsie, I really don't.'

I hugged them both.

'It's OK, my darlings, I'm here now. Nobody is going to hurt you.'

Maybe I was just being obstinate and stupid but, to me in the Four Seasons hotel that night, despite all the evidence, neither Blake nor Amy were real drug addicts. To me, at that time, Mitch and the newspapers had blown the whole thing out of all proportion, just to separate them – and they didn't want to be separated.

Next morning Raye, Amy's manager, joined Mitch, his wife Jane and Amy for breakfast. Giles and I came down and said good morning, but only Amy returned our greeting – she was, as always, happy to see us. I had a bad feeling. We sat at our table and, within minutes, hotel staff appeared from behind us and just stood there, looking. I knew something was wrong. Then, Mitch suddenly jumped up and began to scream at me.

'Your son gave Amy heroin last night.'

I couldn't believe what happened next. Mitch ran over and grabbed Giles by the throat. The staff came running and Amy was pulling at her father and shouting at him to let go. Both Giles and I were in a state of shock. We just sat there, doing and saying nothing, with Mitch holding Giles by the throat. The hotel staff asked if we wanted them to remove "Mister Winehouse" from the premises, but we were too stunned to say anything.

The whole thing seemed to have been staged. The press were there, along with an assortment of so-called "friends" of Amy's. I don't know who they were, they just smirked a lot and hid behind corners. Eventually, I found my voice and spoke to Amy.

'Amy, go get Blake. Your dad's insane.'

Amy ran off, crying. I turned on Mitch. He was holding some kind of tin foil in his hand.

'What the hell are you playing at? You can't say things like that in front of all these people!'

'Your son gave Amy heroin, Georgette. I was given this foil by one of her friends, they say Blake gave it to her.'

I turned on the smirking friends, hiding behind pillars and posts.

'Which friend?'

Nobody answered, they just slid back further into their own shadows. They were enjoying the drama, to them it was a gas. But to me it was a setup!

'Why didn't you come to me, Mitch? We could have dealt with this in private, instead of screaming and shouting in public. What sort of father are you?'

Giles pleaded with the staff of the Four Seasons not to throw Mitch out, despite all the guests on the veranda that morning witnessing the assault.

And all the time, Amy's manager just sat there– and said nothing.

We left the breakfast area and went to Blake. Amy apologised for Mitch's behaviour.

'He's an idiot!'

'Forget about it, Amy. Would you like us to take you two back to London?'

'We'd love you to, mum. But we can't go.'

'Why not?'

'We just can't.'

Amy's manager came into the room. He had dark glasses on and he looked sinister and threatening. I asked him to take them off and he did. I turned on him.

'What the hell is going on here, Raye?'

He just shrugged his shoulders.

'I know things are difficult ..'

'That's an understatement, Raye.'

'Mitch has arranged for a doctor to assess them.'

'What? Who does he think he is, the bloody Godfather?'

Raye just shrugged his shoulders again. I turned to Blake and Amy.

'I want both of you to come with me.'

'Let's go, momsie!'

Amy smiled and immediately began to pack but, before she could finish, a Harley Street specialist called Paul Etlinger arrived. While things were a little chaotic, I saw Raye take a cigarette packet from his pocket and throw it to Blake, even though there were plenty of cigarettes on a table in front of them. I wanted to see what was in the packet, but I couldn't get close to it because the doctor had asked us all to leave the room, except for Blake and Amy. I knew there must be drugs in the packet. I knew it, and Amy's manager was one of the people supplying those drugs.

Giles and I went back to our hotel room and waited. My initial reaction to the cigarette packet was beginning to dilute itself in my mind – surely Amy's manager wouldn't be supplying drugs to her? I must have imagined it. About an hour later, the doctor came to see us and said he had arranged for both Blake and Amy to attend a rehab clinic. I told him Blake didn't need rehabilitation – rehabilitation from what? He said it would be good for Blake and Amy to be together, so I assumed he meant Amy had a problem and Blake needed to be there to help her. When I got the opportunity, I quietly sounded him out about what I had seen in the room and he confirmed that he too had seen the packet being thrown and that I ought to inform Mitch. If a Harley Street doctor had seen it, then it couldn't be my imagination.

After a while, the doctor allowed us to go back to Blake and Amy's room with him. Mitch was already there, alone, in the corridor. The door was locked. We knocked.

'We're just having a bath. Won't be long.'

'Amy darling, it's momsie. Are you both OK?'

'Yes, momsie, we're OK.'

'Is Blake OK?'

'Yes, mum, I'm OK. Don't worry.'

We went back to our room with the doctor and waited. Shortly afterwards, Blake and Amy came to see us. Blake looked terrible, his eyes were dark and he seemed as if he was drunk. Amy, too, was looking out of it.

'Amy and I are going to rehab, mum.'

'I know. Is that what you want?'

The doctor intervened.

'Yes it is. Please, don't get in the way.'

'I'm not getting in the way, but everybody seems to be telling them what to do.'

'It's OK, mum. Amy and I feel it's for the best.'

I began to cry, uncontrollably. I don't know why. Maybe it was because my worst fears had been realised and I was still denying it. Maybe it was because I would be forced to admit to myself that good was bad and that white was black – after all.

'Don't worry, mum. Amy and I will be OK.'

But I couldn't stop crying. I held onto him as tight as I could – what was happening to him? What was happening to my beautiful son? Giles and the doctor prized us apart. Giles took me away from Blake. The doctor tried to calm me.

'You must help me get them to rehab, Georgette. If he sees you crying, he won't go. Please help me. Let him go. You're a good mum, you'll get your son back, I promise you.'

'Will I, doctor?'

'Yes, you will.'

I just wanted him to come home, to be the boy he used to be – once upon a long time ago. They let me hug Blake again, then Amy again. And then I watched them being taken out of the room and down the hotel corridor. Blake called back to me.

'Don't cry, mum. Don't let them see you cry. I love you, OK?'

I followed them, through the hotel and out onto the street. A car was waiting to take them away. Tears rolled down my face. Amy hugged me again.

'Love you, momsie.'

'Love you too.'

Then they were gone. I didn't speak to Mitch, standing there on the pavement beside me, watching the car drive away and thinking whatever it was he thought – feeling whatever it was he felt.

I was still in a kind of bewildered state when we got back home. I told Giles that both the doctor and I had seen Amy's manager passing drugs to Blake – what we believed to be drugs. Giles immediately telephoned Raye and challenged him about it. Raye admitted to getting drugs for Amy on that one occasion, because he wanted to make sure the stuff was the "right gear" and not "rubbish". Amy'd had a brush with death and she didn't need no "bad stuff" in her system right now. He promised

Giles he would never do it again. Giles also told Mitch, Amy's record company and the metropolitan police. Like a fool, I believed the "problem" would now be sorted out.

The rehab clinic was called The Causeway and Blake called me from there.

'Can only make one call, mum .. I love you.'

'I love you too, darling. Don't forget that.'

I cried when he hung the phone up. I wondered would he be OK – would Amy? But they were together, so that was something, at least. I called every day after that, to see how things were going. The staff gave out very little information, which made me angry, but they did say that Blake and Amy were both well. Mitch called me and said he was sorry that things had to be done the way they were.

'But, at least, let's work as a team, for the sake of the young people.'

Shortly after, he rang again to say that Blake and Amy had signed themselves out – only a few days after they signed in. It was a Sunday, Giles had been ringing all day, without being given any information. Then Mitch called to say both Blake and Amy were out, it was about 6.30pm and they'd left The Causeway that morning with a woman called Sarah-Jane and Alex Foden.

'What took you so long to tell us? We may have been able to make them stay.'

I was furious. Why was Mitch informed, but not me? Giles managed to get hold of Blake on his mobile and found out where he was. I convinced Giles to go down to London to see what had happened – and he did, God bless him. It was late and he travelled for several hours to talk to Blake and Amy and try to persuade them to go back to The Causeway, but they wouldn't go. Giles arrived back home at four in the morning, exhausted. He told me Blake and Amy both looked well and happy and I shouldn't worry. They were home in Camden and we'd go see them in a few days.

To sort things out.

When you're so close to the people you love, you only see what you want to see. The signs of drug-addiction were glaring to the rest of the world, but I always saw a different reason for things being the way they were – they were tired, or the press had been particularly nasty, or it was late, or it was raining, or the square on the hypotenuse was no longer equal to the sum of the squares – whatever!

Blake and Amy were so loving, to each other and to me as well. They both loved to be hugged and reassured and I never wanted them to think I wasn't on their side. I never wanted to criticise, I never wanted to part with them on a cross word. Perhaps I was frightened, deep down, that maybe I would never see them again alive and I couldn't bear it if I'd been disloyal – if we'd been estranged in any way. I always wanted Blake to know that I loved him, particularly as I felt I had sometimes let him down at crucial times in his young and vulnerable life.

People will say I'm stupid, but it's difficult to explain the way I felt, unless you've felt like it yourself, for your child – unless you've had the same kind of bond I had with my boy. We had so many foolish little esoteric sayings, Blake and I. If he felt tired or had a headache as a youngster, I would say something silly.

'Have a pill and a poop, my darling.'

It became such a standing joke with us that, whenever after Blake would feel a bit out of sorts, he would always make fun of the silly remarks I made when he was little.

'No, mum, I don't need a pill and a poop.'

And the moon, that was another thing we had – when the moon was full, we always made a wish together, even if we were apart. It was something we did from way back, when he was so small. When he was away from me and the moon was full, I'd go out into the garden and make my wish and I'd feel closer to him – I knew he was doing the same. It was as if some magical silver thread from the silver moon bound us together for that instant – for that moment in time, no matter where we were.

Maybe that's when the seed of suicide began to germinate. Of course, I didn't know it then. But, perhaps the idea of flying in the silver sky with my golden boys started to take its first embryonic shape in my mind then – for a fairytale ending.

But life isn't a fairytale, as I soon found out.

CHAPTER 7
THE COURIER –
THE CONSPIRACY

Amy was supposed to meet me at the hotel in Kensington, to sort out Blake's clothes. But she didn't show up, so mother and I had to do it instead. Kate Anderson came back to see us again and I told her that I had been thinking about making a statement to the police, saying I knew about the payoff to King and had even offered to deliver the money myself. I said I wouldn't involve Amy – or Mitch.

'What do you think?'

The solicitor said the same thing Mitch Winehouse had said, that I would only make matters worse by talking to the police. She said they didn't have enough to convict and Blake didn't need me giving them the evidence they needed.

'Blake will never forgive you if you do that! Let's wait and see what happens.'

I was confused. Maybe she was right – maybe Mitch was right. Maybe things would be OK when the case came to trial and I'd just have to be patient. I didn't know then that, when it came right down to the wire, nobody was going to help my boy. Not his solicitor, not Amy, not Mitch – and not even me.

But there was another thing to worry about right then.

Kate told us that Mitch had withdrawn the bond money which had been posted for Blake's bail. I asked her what that meant.

'It means, even if we do manage to get bail, there's no money for the bond.'

'Why has he done this?'

'It was when I told him of Blake's instruction.'

'What instruction?'

'That I should no longer keep him informed regarding the case, only you and Amy.'

But I knew that wasn't the real reason. It was obvious to me the real reason was because he wanted to keep Blake in prison, where he had control over him – and me.

'What are we going to do, Kate?'

'You need to raise £100,000 before the next hearing, on the twenty-third.'

I needed to speak to Amy. I had to get this sorted. I couldn't allow Blake to be remanded again at the next hearing, just because there wasn't enough money to bail him. I couldn't bear to see that look on his face again – when they took him down!

'Who's money was bonded?'

'It was Amy's.'

'How can Mitch withdraw it?'

'Not sure. That's the message I received .. "we are withdrawing the bail bond".'

I knew very well that "we are" meant "I am". I had to speak to Amy. I was sure Amy could and would sort this out for her husband. Kate spoke off-the-record.

'I must admit, I have a bad feeling about this, Georgette.'

I decided to make a witness statement (copy available) to Kate Anderson about René Butler's visit to my hairdressing salon just a few days earlier, and how the sinister stranger, who nobody believed at the time, gave me a warning that something like this would happen. I wished, right then, that I'd listened to him.

The statement was never used in court.

After Kate left, my mother and I began to make phone calls. By ten o'clock that night, we'd raised £50,000 towards Blake's bail. Amy rang.

'I want to come see you, momsie.'

I told her my mother was with me and where we were.

'Oh, I'd love to meet her ..'

'Come, and we can have dinner. Where are you?'

'I'm with Alex.'

'Will he be coming with you?'

'Would that be OK?'

'Of course, darling. Could you bring some of Blake's clothes, I have a visit on Wednesday.'

'He's got some beautiful clothes .. I'll bring them. Be there soon.'

We waited, but Amy didn't come. I was worried about her, so I called her back and asked if she was OK.

'Yes, I'm OK. See you soon.'

But she didn't sound OK. Shortly after, Mitch rang my mobile. I put the call on loudspeaker again, so my mother could hear. To begin with, he was very polite. He asked if Amy was with me. I told him she wasn't, but she'd be here soon.

'Why have you stopped Blake's bail money, Mitch?'

'I haven't ..'

'Yes you have, his solicitor told me.'

'She's got it wrong. Why would I do that?'

'I've made a statement to her, Mitch.'

He exploded. I could feel the anger coming through the phone. I'm sure if he'd been close to me, he would have hit me.

'What? If that statement is used, Georgette, there'll be big trouble .. not only for you, but for Blake as well!'

'How can Blake be in worse trouble than he's in already?'

'You've been watching too many TV movies. Prison's not so bad .. long as you keep your nose clean.'

'What if it was Amy in prison, Mitch? Would you feel the same way then?'

He must have took this as a counter-threat from me. It wasn't meant like that. I was only trying to explain that he'd want someone to help her, just like I wanted someone to help Blake. The phone went quiet. When Mitch's voice returned, it was quieter, not so violent, but it still seemed latent and full of menace.

'None of this has anything to do with me.'

Now it was my turn to get angry.

'I don't believe you, Mitch. This whole thing stinks and you're right in the middle of it. You're not going to push me around ..'

Mitch hung the phone up. Mother had been writing everything down, like a real-life Miss Marple (all logged). She asked me to ring the police, because of the veiled threats being made. Then she called down to reception and told them not to allow anyone access to our rooms – under any circumstances, just in case.

I telephoned Amy again.

'They won't let me come to you, momsie. They won't tell me anything.'

'Who won't, Amy?'

'I ask what's happening, they just say "don't worry". Please, can you come here?'

I told her I wouldn't be able do that. I said her father had called me and I asked her what was going on where she was. She sounded so strange.

'My mum came today .. it was so unreal. My husband's in jail and she never even mentioned it.'

'Maybe it's difficult for her, Amy.'

'No, it's not. She said she liked my green door. That's all she said .. like Blake doesn't even exist.'

She began to cry.

'Why are they treating me like an idiot?'

'You're not an idiot, Amy.'

'Momsie .. you're the only one I can talk to about our boy. I love him and miss him.'

'I know you do. Why don't you get in a car, Amy, and come over here.'

'I can't. They won't let me.'

'Are you being held against your will, Amy? Amy .. I'll ring the police.'

The phone went dead. I called the police and waited. They called me back, saying they had been round to Amy's flat and she was alright. What was going on? It was past one o'clock in the morning, so I went to bed. Amy called me at two o'clock. She wasn't making very much sense. Then the phone went dead. She called me again at three o'clock – same thing. Then, at four o'clock, she arrived at the hotel. They turned her away. My mother had instructed them not to give anyone access to our rooms.

So they wouldn't.

The last time I saw Blake as a free man was in October 2007. I'd gone down to a hair show in London with some friends and I was staying with

Blake at the flat in Camden. I was so excited, Amy was in Paris and it would be magic to have him all to myself for a while. It wasn't that I didn't love Amy, I did – but mother and son together, it would be like old times again. It was about eight o'clock in the evening when I arrived. I showed him some things I'd bought and we were having a great time. He looked a bit edgy – he said he and Amy had a bit of a row before she left for France. I asked him why and he told me it was because her management had stopped him from going with her.

'But I'm going over tomorrow, mum.'

There was a young woman called Sarah-Jane in the house and that put me off a bit – maybe I was just a little jealous, I wanted to have him to myself. We had so little time together these days. We ordered pizza and sat chatting and I noticed there were some coke tins on the coffee table with holes in them. Sarah-Jane was wrapping up little cubes or balls of stuff in cling-film. I didn't know what she was doing exactly, but I knew it must be something to do with drugs and, if there was ever a time to face up to Blake's addiction, it was right then. I knew I should do something – say something, but what? Should I shout at him, tell him it's wrong, take some responsibility, be responsible? What?

I did nothing.

What would another mother have done? I don't know. I was in a kind of trance, watching the girl, watching Blake. This was happening right in front of me, so surely I couldn't deny it any longer – could I? I couldn't ignore it any longer? What sort of mother was I? I loved my son, yet I was prepared to sit watching him slowly killing himself, denying it all the time and doing nothing about it. I finally spoke. My voice came from somewhere outside myself, as if it was someone else speaking.

'Are they drugs?'

'Mum ..'

'Are they, Blake?'

'Mum, please ..'

'I love you Blake .. if you die, then I'll die. Can't you see that?'

'You always do this. You always make me feel guilty!'

We faced each other for a moment, then he hugged me. My arms were limp around him for a second, just a second. Then I hugged him back.

The young woman took all the stuff away and it was like it hadn't happened. It wasn't happening. I had imagined it. I didn't want to make him feel guilty, I wanted him to love me, to know I loved him. How would it be if I had a big argument with him now, and he died? Love! Guilt! Both are very strong emotions – like life and death, they're two sides of the same coin.

Next morning, Blake was back to normal. My Blake was back. We had some fun and thoughts of the night before faded.

'Make me a cup of tea, mum, and you can use the hoover if you like. I know how much you like the sound of the hoover.'

'Cheeky devil!'

'And could you run me a bath. No-one runs a bath like you, mum.'

And I did, I went upstairs and ran him a bath. But, while Blake was in the bathroom, I could hear him making choking noises.

'Blake .. are you OK?'

'Yes mum, don't worry.'

I thought he was just clearing his throat, so I went down to the kitchen to make the tea and I saw something on the table. I know now it was a piece of "rock" – I didn't know what it was then. I took it to the bathroom with the tea.

'Blake, I found this on the table ..'

As I came into the bathroom, I saw Blake swallowing all the little cling-film parcels the young woman had made the night before. He was making choking noises with every ball he swallowed. Somehow, I knew what was happened. Fear and panic filled me. I dropped the tea, and the rock.

'Blake, please .. don't do this.'

'Go away, mum!'

'Please, come home with me now.'

'Mum, you're making me nervous.'

'Please! Please!'

'Stop talking, mum!'

Sarah-Jane, the young woman, came and took me away from the bathroom. I waited for Blake to come down stairs, so I could plead with him again, so I could beg him to come home with me – even for just a few days. But a car came to take him to the airport. He gave me a lift to King's Cross. We hardly spoke. My heart was filled with dread. What if the cling-film broke inside him? I looked at him, as he sat silently beside me in the car. I just saw Blake – I didn't see what was inside him. Was I frightened to look? Was I a coward?

I believed that Blake was what they call in that world, a "mule". He was Amy's mule, taking drugs over to her in Paris, where she wouldn't have the same connections she had in London. I buried my face in my hands to try to keep out the reality of the situation. We quickly arrived at King's Cross and I got out of the car. I was afraid to hug him, in case I burst one of the little packets that were inside him. He kissed me and smiled.

'Smile, Mum. You're beautiful when you smile.'

The car moved away from me. I just stood there and watched it go, in slow-motion, like in a dream. I couldn't smile. Instead, tears ran down my face and I pleaded with God to keep my son alive. I didn't know then that I would eventually plead with the same God to help me kill the same son.

On my way home, I telephoned a man called Tom, who was Amy's band manager.

'Tom, Blake is on his way. Could you please make sure Amy meets him at the airport?'

'I'll try. She's in bed.'

'Please wake her, tell her Blake is arriving soon.'

'I'll try. It's not east getting Amy out of bed.'

'Please Tom, promise me that someone will be there to meet him.'

'I promise.'

I needed to know if Blake arrived safely. I had to know. I couldn't rest till I knew! Several hours later, Tom telephoned. Blake had arrived OK. Amy didn't meet him, but they were together now and they were both happy.

'Thank you, Lord!'

So far so good. But, when Blake and Amy got back to London in October, the media were printing more terrible things about them. I telephoned again and Amy tried to reassure me again.

'I told you, momsie, it's all bollocks!'

But it was going from bad to worse in the press. The GBH charge was hanging over Blake's head and the newspapers and magazines were making a meal of it. Blake was getting nervous about it, believing that all the bad stuff being said would make things difficult for him in court. Giles told him not to worry, the prisons were already overcrowded and he'd be OK – probably get community service or something. Blake hoped he was right. So did I. It's not that I thought the assault on James King was trivial in any way. No, it was terrible. If one of my boys had been hurt like that, I would have wanted justice. I realised that justice had to be done, but I wanted real justice, fair-and-square justice, not lynch-mob justice.

So, when Blake and Amy called me one night and said they had been approached by a friend of James King and a sum of money was mentioned to ensure King didn't turn up in court, I felt relieved and worried at the same time. I didn't quite know what to say to them.

'What do you think, mum?'

'I don't know, Blake. It's breaking the law, isn't it?'

'I mentioned it to my solicitor, mum. She said to find out as much as possible.'

'Maybe we should let the police know?'

It was just a chat like that, just words between us. I don't think any of us realised the implications of those words. I don't believe we knew that what was being suggested was wrong. We just wanted the whole thing to go away and maybe this would suit everyone – maybe, this way, everyone could be a winner.

'Perhaps .. if you like, I could hand over the money for you?'

'No, momsie, you can't do it. Blake and I won't let you do that.'

'I don't mind, Amy.'

'No, momsie! We'll sort it out.'

'Amy .. are you sure it'll be OK?'

'I hate King, momsie .. but, it'll be alright.'

'OK, darling, just be careful.'

After thinking about it, it seemed to be the perfect solution. If King was happy to take the money, then where was the harm? That way, Amy could keep her sailor and nobody got hurt. It was easy to justify.

Until the unpredictable drug-dealer arrived with the warning.

There were four men involved in the deal to pay off James King, to make sure he didn't turn up for the GBH trial. Blake, Michael Brown, James Kennedy and Anthony Kelly – and, of course, King himself. At the end of October, Kelly and Kennedy had tried to sell some footage of the assault, that they'd gotten from the pub CCTV, to the newspapers on King's behalf. But there were no buyers, because the newspapers knew that the footage would be available for free after the trial. One of those newspapers was the Daily Mirror and the reporter they approached was a man called Stephen Moyes. When they couldn't sell the assault footage, Kelly and Kennedy came up with the payoff idea for King and approached Blake and Amy with it.

The deal was agreed and £8,000 was withdrawn from Amy's account to give to Kelly as "walking around" money, for when he took King abroad on holiday, "out of the way". The total amount to be paid was £200,000 – but only £5,000 was ever actually handed over. Then Kelly got greedy – he wanted more. He went back to Stephen Moyes and told him about the payoff deal. Moyes agreed to pay him another £5,000 to set up a sting.

Moyes hired a private investigator called Steve Grayson, who placed two covert cameras in a house where Anthony Kelly arranged to meet James King. He told King on camera that Blake had agreed to the payoff and secretly taped King admitting that he was prepared to withdraw his allegations for the money and not turn up in court. One of the cameras was planted in a handbag and the other in a light sensor. When the meeting ended, Moyes and Grayson retrieved the cameras, only to find that one of them had never been switched on and only footage from the handbag camera was available. King had agreed to accept the payoff of his own free will, without any threats or intimidation. Blake was not at the meeting, but he was implicated by Kelly for the benefit of the hidden cameras.

Moyes decided to call in the metropolitan police and, before the night came to make the payoff, the police made their move. I believed Mitch was tipped off by Moyes, so he could get Amy out of the way, before Moyes went over to the flat in Camden with a cameraman, to get an exclusive on Blake's arrest for the Daily Mirror. Kelly and Kennedy were being arrested outside a pub in London, King was arrested in Derby and Brown gave himself up a few days later. The police went to Camden and kicked the door in, looking for Blake, who would have been there, alone – should have been there alone. But wasn't.

Blake did go home to Camden that night, but left again before the police arrived, to go to Alex Foden's flat. Stephen Moyes followed him and, within a few minutes, police arrived at the Amiga Buildings in Roach Road E3. Mitch and Amy were there with Alex. Blake suspected nothing. It seemed quite obvious to me that Mitch had taken Amy out to dinner to get her out of Camden. I believed he knew the police were coming and he expected Blake to be there, not at Alex's flat.

These are the facts as I knew them, as I believed them to be at the time, not from any newspaper report or witness statement, but as I knew them, as a mother – as I saw them, as a mother – as I concluded in my own mind, as a mother, what was happening to the son I loved so much.

What I also knew was that Mitch Winehouse was giving an exclusive interview (on record) to Stephen Moyes of the Daily Mirror, only hours after Blake was arrested. In that interview, he told Moyes he hoped Blake went to prison, it would be the best thing that could happen – that way, he could save Amy.

CHAPTER 8
A WARNING – ARREST

On Sunday, 4th November 2007, I'd received a telephone call from a strange sounding man who said his name was René Butler. He asked me if I knew there was a deal going down to pay off James King. I refused to comment – I didn't know who he was, he could be anybody, police even.

'I need to see you, it's about Blake's forthcoming trial.'

He said a sinister plot was being hatched by certain people and something real bad was going to happen to Blake. I was worried. If this man knew about the payoff, who else knew? Who wanted to hurt Blake?

'Who are you? What do you want?'

'I told you, my name is René Butler. I'm a friend of Blake's.'

He claimed he'd met Blake about a year previously and they had a drink together. He told me he liked Blake and he wasn't prepared to stand back and allow that kind of stuff to happen to him. He was worried in case I was taping the conversation and details of what he was saying might get back to the wrong people. He said he wanted me to know that friends of Amy's father had an agenda to sabotage Blake's trial for GBH. He also told me he was willing to share information with me about a newspaper that was involved and how Mitch was going to make money out of selling Blake to that newspaper. He emphasised that he was risking a great deal by contacting me with this information.

I asked the man what he wanted out of all this and he said he wanted nothing. He said we needed to meet up, as he couldn't tell me anything else over the phone. He said we had to do it urgently, but I was nervous of him, suspicious, apprehensive.

'I'll call you back, OK?'

'You have to protect your son!'

After I hung up, I immediately telephoned Blake and Amy and told them about the strange conversation with this man called René Butler, if that was indeed, his real name. Blake wasn't too concerned and said he was probably just a reporter looking for information and I should be very careful.

'Meet him, mum. But be clever and tell him nothing. Tape what he has to say, OK!'

I called René Butler back and it was arranged that we should meet the following Tuesday at 4.00pm at my salon. He would then supply me with sufficient evidence to support what he was saying. What was going on? This was like some second-rate spy movie. It couldn't really be happening. Clandestine meetings, taping conversations – really!

But, just in case, I arranged for one of my staff from the salon, Tracy Taylor, to stay with me on Tuesday, after I'd closed up the shop. We waited. A white man arrived at 4.00pm sharp. He was about thirty years old, with a baby-face and a stocky build. He was dressed casually, but looked sinister to me. Tracy went to make him a cup of coffee, while he told me he was putting himself at risk by coming to the salon to see me. He wanted to know if I was taping the conversation and I assured him I wasn't. I don't think he believed me and he kept looking round, to see where Tracy was. He was obviously wary of someone else being in the salon with me, because he began to draw something on a piece of paper. He whispered that it was a diagram of the people who were plotting Blake's downfall. He drew a kind of semi-circle, which he said represented the newspaper that was involved. To the left of it he drew what looked like a big sun, and in the middle he wrote the word "mitch". He said this was the main man who was trying to get Blake set up. He whispered to me that Amy's father was afraid Blake might get off the GBH charge and, if that happened, he'd never get rid of him. The agenda was to trash the forthcoming trial and get Blake for something bigger.

He asked me if Blake was going to America the following Wednesday, where Amy was due to perform. He said if Blake was found in possession of drugs in the US, he'd get sent down for ten years. This really frightened me.

He then wrote the words "snitch" and "bitch" on either side of the diagram with "mitch" in the centre. I asked him what those words meant and he said it was well known that Mitch gave a third party bits of dirt about Blake whenever he could, all the stuff about Blake being a notorious drug-addict and white slave-trader, who was killing Amy deliberately, which that person then sold to the newspapers. That third party was a cab driver who worked the same Kent rank as Mitch and was known by everybody as "mitch's bitch". Just then, Tracy came back with the cup of coffee and she saw the diagram, before he could hide it from her (she will confirm this). Then she had to go, leaving me alone in the salon with the mysterious René Butler. I felt uneasy and a bit silly at the same time. "I'm a hairdresser", I thought to myself, "not a gangster!".

René, if that was his name, then asked me for something exclusive. I told him that, when Blake was younger, he wanted to become a priest. This didn't satisfy him, it wasn't enough. I then told him that everyone knew who was supplying Blake and Amy with drugs. Those people were hanging around all the time and Mitch knew who they were, Amy's management knew who they were and nobody did anything about it. I told him he could quote me, but he began to get more and more agitated. He said it wasn't enough, he said he'd given me all this information and that he was getting "fuck all" in return. I said he hadn't given me any real evidence, just a vague drawing that could mean anything. His language and manner were becoming aggressive and I began to get frightened. I asked him to leave, but he wouldn't go. Just then, a car pulled up outside the salon and René got nervous and left quickly. But he didn't go away, he stayed outside on the street for about twenty minutes, watching me through the window. I could see him watching me and I didn't know what to do. I was very scared. I thought about ringing Giles and having him come get me, but I had convinced myself that this man was a drug-dealer and what if he had a gun or a knife? I didn't want Giles getting hurt. So I waited. And waited. My imagination was running away with me, was somebody going to kill Blake? Blake's not a gangster, he's Blake – my son! Finally, René Butler left and I locked up immediately and ran to my car and drove off as quickly as I could.

When I got home, I rang René Butler again from my landline phone and used my mobile to record the conversation (recording available). I wanted to try to find out exactly who he was. But he wouldn't tell me and I never did find out. He was angry and said he believed I'd taped the conversation at the salon. I promised him I hadn't. He said it was all a "waste of space" because he didn't get anything from me. I reminded him that he'd said he wanted nothing in return. I don't know if this upset him or not, but he hung up and I decided to leave it so, at least for now.

After that conversation, I telephoned Blake and Amy again and told them everything that had went on in the salon. I begged them not to go to America the following Wednesday, in case anything happened to Blake.

'Please Amy, promise me you won't go!'

'No we won't, momsie, I promise you.'

'Promise, Blake! Promise you won't go to the States!'

'I promise you, mum, Amy and I will stay at home.'

'If anything happened over there, I'd never get you back.'

I was relieved. But Amy said she couldn't believe her father would do anything to hurt Blake or have him put in prison. Blake believed her and the warning was ignored. There wasn't long to go to the trial, so I relaxed and tried to put the sinister rendezvous at the salon out of my mind. After all, this wasn't the first so-called conspiracy – ever since Blake and Amy got married, there were conspiracy theories – rumours of signed agreements so Blake could never benefit if anything happened to Amy, rumours of Blake being a secret slave-trader and having a harem, rumours of orgies and porgies and puddings and pie – all sorts of weird stuff. I should have been more alert, I never suspected anything about the payoff to King – I didn't know when it was going to take place and I thought the warning was to do with America. And, now that both of them had promised not to go –

You see, it wasn't just Mitch who didn't want Blake and Amy to be together. As soon as Amy became a big star, all sorts of vested interests got involved – all sorts of people, out to make some money, came creeping out of the woodwork and began to peddle their versions of the truth. Everyone had an agenda, to sell newspapers, to sell records, to sell rumours. Some rumours were lies – but some were true!

The next time I spoke to René Butler was after Blake had been arrested, I wanted to thank him for the warning and to apologise for not acting on it – but it was too late then.

He never contacted me again.

Blake was arrested on charges of conspiracy to pervert the course of justice at 18.35 hours on Thursday 8th November 2007 – two days after my meeting with René .

You know the rest.

I did confront Mitch Winehouse with the conversation I had with René Butler in the salon that night. He said if I told the police or Blake's lawyers about it, he'd sue me.

I got up really early on Wednesday 14th November. I was already in London and I was on a high – visiting Blake at 2.00pm. I went over my checklist a thousand times – identification, visiting order, other paperwork, taxi booked, stuff for Blake – I checked again, to make sure I had the right time and date. The minutes moved so slowly, I should have stayed in bed a bit longer, I checked the paperwork again, had another cup of coffee. My mother was with me and she tried to calm me down. I did my best to look nice, so Blake would at least feel that I was OK. I couldn't let him see how I really felt. I used some perfume he'd bought me for Christmas and I hoped he'd remember it.

The taxi arrived at 1.00pm. I couldn't be late! I had no idea how the system worked at Pentonville and I didn't want to leave anything to chance. We had to go round the back of the prison to book in, due to the number of press people outside. My stomach was churning. I remember the huge metal doors, we had to knock, the press were everywhere, we had bags of things for Blake, it was chaos. After a few minutes, an officer came and let us in and it was calmer inside. We had to hand over the presents we'd brought so they could be searched before being given to Blake. Welcome to prison life!

But the officers were nice to us on this occasion and even made us coffee. They told us Amy was on her way. I knew Blake would be so pleased to see her. The officers saw how nervous I was and tried to reassure me that Blake was alright.

'He's in the hospital wing.'

'Why is he there?'

'It's the best place for him. We can monitor him there.'

'Has he been in trouble?'

'No, Mrs Civil, Blake is fine. I promise you.'

I began to cry again. That's all I ever seemed to be doing. The pain in my chest was so tight, I was having difficulty breathing. My mother tried to calm me again.

'Don't cry, Georgette, we'll be seeing him in a few minutes.'

'I know. You're right.'

One of the prison officers gave me a cigarette, which I thought was such a kind gesture at the time. Two doctors arrived. They wanted to see me before I went in, to get some background information, they said. They also tried to reassure me that Blake was fine and I shouldn't worry. That's when I began to cry again. I was full of emotion and indescribable pain. They gave me time to compose myself and then, when I was ready, we went in.

My mind was in turmoil. I kept telling myself to be strong and brave, not to cry. I'd be hugging my son in a few minutes and I had to be a rock for him! The hospital area was hot and clean. I don't think I've ever seen a place so clean. It was kind of like the clean you imagine heaven to be, so white and bright – scarily clean, if that's possible. We were taken into a large room, with a table and four chairs. A prison officer sat at the table.

'I have to sit in, I'm sorry. I hope you understand.'

'Yes .. of course.'

You say you understand, but you don't. You just say "yes" to everything, in case you cause a problem and they won't let you see your boy. Mother and I sat at the table.

'Blake will be here soon.'

Mother chatted to the officer, while I started to cry again. Mentally, I kept screaming at myself, "for God's sake, pull yourself together, if he sees you now, you'll just upset him".

They brought him into the room and I stood and ran to him. The tears were uncontrollable now, as I hugged and hugged him – my boy, my beautiful darling boy.

'I love you!'

I told him, over and over again. Even my mother was crying now. He smiled.

'I'm staying in the hospital wing for a few weeks ..'

But his eyes looked sad and haunted – dark and sunken. I couldn't even imagine what he must be going through. He tried so hard to look upbeat and told us he was OK. He looked just like the hospital area, so very clean. I've never seen anyone look so clean – isn't it silly, how these things stick in your head? The officer allowed him to have a cigarette and we told him about the things we'd brought and tried to joke about the underwear, because mother was in charge of that. We all laughed and the laughter took the pain away, at least for a little while, for a few minutes. But the sorrow in Blake's eyes could not be drowned out by any amount of laughing. I will remember it forever.

After about half an hour, a doctor came to us.

'Amy's here, Blake,'

He got so excited, I thought he was going to have a heart attack.

'Oh, mum .. Amy's here!'

'That's wonderful, darling.'

The officer had to calm him down, he was so happy. She ran to him as soon as she came into the room. They hugged each other and cried. She kept holding his face and kissing him.

'You're so handsome, my handsome sailor ..'

'Amy, mum's here.'

'Hi, momsie.'

'This is Blake's grandma, Amy.'

'Hi, grandma.'

We hugged and kissed. She hugged and kissed my mother.

They were so happy in the moment, in the short time they had together. But Amy looked unkempt, in contrast to Blake, who looked so clean. "Oh Amy darling", I thought to myself. I did love her! She looked vulnerable and lonely. I felt I knew her so well, she needed Blake just like I did. And Blake needed Amy. He proved his love by keeping her safe, by keeping her out of the conspiracy, by taking all the blame himself. I looked at her and I felt so sad. What would happen to her in a place like this? Maybe Blake knew what he was doing after all. For the first time I thought, maybe this is the way it has to be. I hugged her again.

'I'm so pleased you came, Amy.'

'Look at our boy, momsie. Doesn't he look so handsome?'

Yes, he was our boy. And yes, he was so handsome. We shared our feelings in that prison hospital, Amy and I, and we were so close in our mutual love for Blake. She kept stroking his face and kissing him and Blake was so happy to be with her. It made me cry again – why do we cry when we see such love? Or maybe it was just me feeling guilty again – we'd all played our part, but only Blake was paying the price.

'Darling, grandma and I will go outside for a while, so you and Amy can have some time together.'

It was an excuse to hide my tears.

'Thanks, mum.'

'Oh, momsie, you don't have to go ..'

Back then, that was Amy – so understanding. She loved him as much as I did, yet she was thinking of me and my short time with him.

'No, darling, you need to be together.'

I kissed him, then mother and I went outside.

'He looks so thin, I could feel his ribs ..'

'I know, Georgette, but he's getting the best treatment possible.'

The doctors joined us again, while we waited to go back into the room. One of them made a comment.

'Blake is so polite. He's not the person the press have made him out to be.'

This was such a joy for me to hear, a prison doctor confirming how nice a person Blake really was – not calling him a "junkie" or a "loser", but a human being with a heart and soul.

'Will he be OK, doctor?'

'Yes, he will. Blake has an inner strength. He'll get through this. It's hard, but he will.'

'He will .. won't he?'

'He has to.'

I found myself plea-bargaining with God again. Please make him be alright and I'll do this, or I'll do that. I plea-bargained all the time, making promises I knew I couldn't or wouldn't keep, but I continued to do it – I was doing it again now. And, if I wasn't pleading, I was crying!

There has to be a reason for such pain and misery. We have to learn from it, surely? I didn't know then what it was I had to learn – that came later. All I felt then was overwhelming love for my boy, who was in trouble.

He looked happier when we went back in. Amy did too. I continued with the visit, showing as much strength as I could, trying to pretend everything was OK, laughing and smiling, though my heart was breaking, living the lie. The officer soon called time and my heart began to race again.

'Do I have to go?'

'Sorry, yes you do.'

We stood up together and each of us, in turn, hugged Blake. I cried again. Amy held me.

'Oh, momsie, please don't cry.'

But I couldn't keep the pretence up any longer. My heart broke. I wanted to hold onto him, to stay there with him, to take his pain away –

'Darling, remember the full moon ..'

'I will, mum. Look after Amy for me.'

'Of course.'

'We'll look after each other, sailor .. till you come home.'

Then he was led away. My boy. Not a "junkie" or a "loser", but my boy. And part of me went with him.

Addiction is so cruel. It laughs at love. It mocks you, taunts you, it tells you it's got your son and asks you what you're going to do about it. It has you in the palm of its hand and it can destroy you just as easily as it can destroy the person who's addicted. And it does! You wonder how you can compete with it, especially if you deny it, as I was doing. You try to face it, but it's too ugly, you can't look at it for long. You turn away, and it grows stronger. Denial is as evil as the addiction itself. They feed off each other. They feed off fear. They feed off love!

We left the prison.

I would make many more visits to Pentonville and other places of detention. I didn't know it then, but the ritual would become part of my life for the next two and a half years. And there was a whole new set of rules I would have to learn – to survive it.

CHAPTER 9
PENTONVILLE

Sadly, my relationship with Amy began to deteriorate after Blake was arrested and sent to Pentonville. We were in touch, we saw each other in court, in the barrister's chambers and we'd have a smoke together, we'd write notes to Blake together. I did love her, because Blake did – but, to me, it seemed she was lost. They were both lost in their own way, Amy and Blake. Blake had lost his freedom, but Amy had lost herself. She continued on a downhill spiral after Blake's arrest. She was in the papers almost every day it seemed, looking drunk, or drugged, or wasted and the worst-for-wear – and it was still all Blake's fault, despite the fact that he was locked up in Pentonville.

My first impression of Pentonville, after that initial visit where everything was clean and white, soon dissipated. I came to know it as a horrible place, really. My next visiting day was on a Monday. I came on my own, without my mother. I sat in first class on the train, even though I didn't have a first class ticket. It signified to me, in some strange way, that I was somehow a respectable woman, not a failed mother going to visit her son in prison. I was on a high, so excited at the prospect of seeing Blake again. We'd have two hours together, the most important two hours in the day.

I didn't have a clue what to do or where to go when I got to the prison. I was searched and checked so many times before they let me through. I was disorientated and confused and the euphoria of the train soon left me, after hair and body searches, with even my shoes and socks removed. I had to allow a dog to smell me to make sure I wasn't smuggling in drugs. It was all so degrading, so untrusting, so cold. Then I met a very helpful woman who knew the ropes. She showed me where to put my bag and coat and scarf, how to pay a pound for a locker, how to conform to the ritual of prison visiting. I was so glad to have her help,

I needed a friend in the emotional labyrinth of Pentonville security procedures. I was then directed into line with all the other visitors. I listened to them chatting, while we waited. They all seemed so happy and chirpy. But the brutality of the admittance routine had made me sad and depressed. It was a routine I would have to go through time and time again, over the next seven months.

After a few visits, I got used to it – as used to it as anyone could get. I would be given a number, which corresponded with a number on one of the tables in the visiting room. Then I would wait. Visiting time always started at 2.00pm. I would see the prisoners coming up the stairs in their orange tops, with their individual numbers on them, then being directed to their table by the prison officers. I would tell myself to be strong and not to cry. Then I would see Blake, his head first, his smiling face, and then the rest of him – and the tears would always fall.

'Hi, mum.'

He would shout over to me. I'd want to run to him, to hug and kiss him. The officers would tell me to wait at the table. I wouldn't be able to wait. I'd wonder why I was the only one crying, what was wrong with me, why did I always have to cry? Then he'd be at the table and I could hug and kiss him.

I always brought things for him, which were always taken away from me, so I could never have the pleasure of giving them to him myself. We'd talk about so many things – there were so many things to be talked about in the two short hours we shared . I would stop crying and start smiling and we would be happy together – for the brief little time that flew past so quickly. Blake was always positive and upbeat. I know now it was just a front, he was doing it for me, to help me cope – and I tried to do it for him, without much success. And each time I had to leave, I would leave a little piece of myself behind.

It wasn't long before I began to get phone calls from Blake, asking me to put fifty pounds into this account and fifty pounds into that account – accounts which were in the names of people I didn't know. I asked him why he wanted me to do this and he told me not to worry, it was just for phone calls. So I did it. Then, one night, a man telephoned me and said he wanted five hundred pounds by the next day.

'I rang Amy, but she's not answering her phone. So I thought you would do it.'

'Why do you want so much?'

'You know how it is.'

'No, I don't.'

'Five hundred .. by tomorrow, please.'

I knew this couldn't be for phone calls, so I rang Amy.

'Oh, I'm so angry that happened. Leave it with me, momsie.'

'What's going on, Amy?'

'Please don't worry. I'm so angry you've been involved. I'll sort it out.'

'What's the money for, Amy?'

'Leave it with me, I'll make sure it gets paid. Have you paid out any more?'

'Yes, but ..'

'I'll send you a cheque.'

'I don't want your money, Amy. Is Blake OK?'

'Yes. Never pay out any more money, momsie. Leave it to me.'

That was the end of the conversation. Why were we paying this money? What were we paying for, and who were we paying it to? I was too naive to understand – I thought maybe it was protection money or something, who knows? Until it eventually dawned on me many months later – we were paying for drugs.(evidence of payments available).

As I continued to see Blake on remand in Pentonville, my sadness grew. I didn't know he wasn't getting much help for his drug addiction. On the contrary, his addiction was being fed from the inside and the outside. I was never contacted for a large amount of money again, but I continued to send £50 cheques to his account in prison and to people on the outside. I felt really confused inside about it, but I always convinced myself, in the end, that it was for the phone and, as long as he had his phone and called me, that was justification enough. I knew very well he was getting drugs, but I told myself it could only be small amounts and, in a place like that, you needed something. I made excuse after excuse, knowing full well I was fooling myself, but I still paid the money. You do things like that for your children, don't you? When they ask you face to face in a prison visiting room, or on telephone from a prison cell.

Just as my sadness at the situation was growing, Blake's sadness was also growing, for a different reason. Amy never came, nor wrote, and he felt very alone. I didn't comment on this to him, in case I upset him, and I always tried to support her, to make excuses for her, despite my real feelings. On one particular visit, he was more upset than usual.

'I can't understand why Amy never visits, mum .. why she never writes.'

He was almost in tears. I didn't know what to say. I loved Amy, but the drugs were making her unreliable. That's what I saw happening, the drugs were changing her. As well as that, I believed her family and her management were against her visiting Blake. I believed they thought this time apart would break Amy and Blake up – and that's what everybody wanted, wasn't it? I was angry about this. I tried to bury my anger and hurt when I was with Blake, for his sake, but it was eating me up inside. Here I was, trying to deal with my own guilt and failings, trying to cope with my son in prison, and now I was trying and failing to understand why Amy was letting Blake down like this. She would book visits, but never turn up. She never wrote. They must have been communicating in some way, in order to arrange the payments for drugs, but that wasn't a substitute for personal, human, loving contact – or maybe it was!

'Darling, why did you never tell the truth about the conspiracy?'

'What sort of a husband would that make me, mum? Daydreams would do it for you, wouldn't he?'

'I believe he would. The difference is, I would have been there for him.'

'But, you're not an addict, are you?'

'No, darling, I'm not.'

I began to hate those prison visits. It was a schizophrenic thing, I loved them because they allowed me to see Blake, but I hated them because I knew it should have been Amy visiting Blake, not me all the time. I wondered who the money went to, that was paid into the unfamiliar accounts – was it prison officers? Were they running a protection racket? When I was with Blake, I couldn't help looking at the officers guarding the prisoners and wondering if they were involved – if the guards were as guilty as the men they were watching over. Was there any real difference between the two groups? What chance had my son got in such a system? Would he be worse when he came out than when he went in? If he was acquitted when he finally came to trial, would his time on remand have damaged him irrevocably? If so, where was the justice in that? If he was found guilty and had to go back, what further damage would be done?

Amy continued to book visits and fail to turn up. I would ring her when I knew she had a visit.

'Hi, Amy. Are you seeing Blake today?'

'Yes, momsie.'

'Good girl. Give him my love and have a nice visit.'

'Will do. Talk later.'

I would ring her management and beg them to make sure she went.

'Make sure the car is there.'

'Will do, but you know Amy.'

'Please try.'

'We will.'

I would ring Amy again. I would beg her to go. I would try to make her visualize how it was for Blake, getting excited that she was coming to see him, then sitting there all alone in the visiting room and being taken back to his cell disappointed. Was it any wonder he needed a few drugs?

'Promise me, Amy.'

'I promise, momsie.'

'Please don't let him down, Amy. If you can't go, I'll go instead.'

'No, momsie. I'm really looking forward to it. I'll give him your love.'

At two o'clock, I'd call her management, to see if she'd gone yet.

'No, Georgette. But don't worry, the car is there.'

I'd ring again at 2.15pm. No answer. That was always bad news. I'd ring again at 2.30pm and again at 3.00pm – always the same. Amy would not be going. I would get so upset, imagining Blake sitting there, waiting and watching for her. Knowing, with each passing minute, that she wasn't going to turn up again. How cruel and cold and selfish, I thought.

I resented Amy for that. But, was she entirely responsible? Did she fully understand the pain she was causing, not only to Blake, but to me? I could have gone in her place, even though he needed to see his wife, not his mother again. The animosity I felt towards Amy grew with each passing week. In my mind I called her a selfish bitch. I visualized myself telling her "he gave you your freedom and this is how you pay him back". The anger and frustration built up, my son was waiting all alone in that prison, she didn't deserve his love – nor mine. I tried to make excuses for her behaviour, but that didn't work anymore. Addict or no addict, I thought, it was unreasonable and couldn't be excused. The night before a visit she'd be out getting drunk or wasted until four, or five, or six in the morning. And a "close source" would tell the press it was all because of Blake.

But, to me, Amy only had her freedom because of Blake. She could only have her nights out because of Blake. She could only party with her friends because of Blake. He gave her freedom and that freedom locked the rest of us up in hell. And she didn't seem to care. I kept changing my mind about Amy every five minutes – she did love Blake, she didn't love Blake. I remembered how close they were and how loving they looked when they were together and I saw how uncaring she seemed when they were apart. I visited my son every week and every week I had to look at the pain inflicted by Amy through her absence, and the torment inflicted by "close sources" through the media stories that were appearing daily. It all came to a head inside me. I rang Amy.

'Amy, why didn't you go see Blake today?'

'I'm not well, momsie.'

'Not well? You were out last night, Amy.'

'I'm not well.'

'Listen to me, Amy, if it wasn't for Blake you'd be in prison too.'

'I love Blake, you know I do.'

'Well, bloody show it then! Be a wife and visit him!'

'I am his wife.'

'You're not behaving like it!'

She went quiet. I could hear noises in the background, banging noises and a can being pierced. I asked her what the noises were, even though I knew.

'We're putting up pictures.'

'Don't treat me like an idiot, Amy. Someone's smoking cocaine.'

Everything went quiet in the background.

'No .. they're not.'

'For God's sake .. sort yourself out, Amy!'

I don't know who was there with her, she wouldn't say. Some of the many "friends" who frequented the flat in Camden. I told her they weren't really her friends and that was the first real fight we'd ever had, Amy and I, shouting at each other down the phone like that. I didn't want to fight with her, I knew she had her own problems to deal with, her own demons to face, but I believed it was the only way to make her come to her senses, as far as Blake was concerned. But it was pointless, she wasn't going to listen.

'Will you be seeing Blake on Monday?'

'Yes, I promise.'

'If you don't, Amy, I'll book all the visits up .. I promise you that! I won't let you hurt him anymore.'

'We both love Blake, momsie, you and me .. that's why we're fighting. That's the reason for all this emotion.'

There it was again – one minute I was angry and the next minute I was reassured. I couldn't make up my mind what to think – I couldn't figure her out. The thing is, you can't stay mad at Amy for long. So, I trusted her again – and loved her.

'Goodnight, Amy. God bless.'

'Love you, momsie.'

There were times I thought I should telephone Mitch, but what would he do? According to the media, Amy had more security than the Queen. So, who was turning a blind eye? True to form, next day the papers had pictures of her all over the place – and it was, of course, Blake's fault.

But Amy did eventually get away from her minders and go to Pentonville. Blake was sad when he told me about the visit.

'She looks terrible, mum, all cuts on her arms .. and she slept through most of it .. drugs do that to you. I love her so much, but it's hard to know what to do.'

How could I help him? A part of me wanted to hate her, but another part of me loved her. The drugs always got in the way, always came between us, laughed at me for being a fool. I saw that Blake had also cut his arms.

'What happened, darling?'

'It relieves the pain, mum.'

I didn't understand. I would kiss him and smile and tell him how much he meant to me and how I loved him, but he knew all that already. He wanted his wife, he wanted Amy. But Amy had been kidnapped by a combination of drugs and dominance.

Then they reported in the papers that she was having an affair. It was a Sunday morning headline. I was distraught. How would this affect Blake? They'd all be laughing at him in Pentonville. The phone began to ring. First it was Kate the solicitor, wanting to know if we'd seen the newspaper, then the reporters began to call. It was a nightmare. I had to speak to Blake. Giles said the prison wouldn't allow me to talk to him, Kate Anderson said it would be difficult.

'It's Sunday, Georgette, you might not get anywhere.'

'I don't care what day it is, Kate, I need to speak to him.'

I telephoned and, to my surprise, they got Blake for me and put him in an office so we could talk privately.

'You've seen it then, mum?'

'Yes, darling, I have.'

'Do you believe it?'

'I don't know, do you?'

'I'm trying to get hold of Amy.'

'I'm coming tomorrow, you know that, don't you?'

'I feel as if my heart's breaking, mum.'

An officer came on the phone and told me not to worry, they would make sure he was OK and they'd try to help him get hold of Amy. That's the nicest thing Pentonville ever did for me – the only thing.

The whole world knew about my son's arrest, and now the whole world believed his wife was cheating on him – and they still blamed him. I visited him the next day. He looked so sad. He had a bandage on his wrist. I held it.

'Oh, my darling ..'

'Don't, mum ..'

His face was full of pain and he was trying hard to hold back the tears.

I knew if I cried, he would too. Giles had made me promise I'd be strong, and I did try. It was hard – but I did it for Blake.

'Do you believe all this shit in the media, mum?'

'No darling, but it sells newspapers.'

'Amy loves me, you know that.'

'Yes, I do.'

I said these things to make him feel better, but I didn't know if what the papers said was true, or if Amy really loved him.

'They blame me all the time, mum. But, the thing is, Amy was on drugs before I came on the scene. It just got worse after we got together. Try to get her away from where Alex lives, mum, that's a bad place.'

'Why do you let them blame you, Blake?'

'It's easier to say it's my fault. She's the star, I'm a nobody. Her career is more important than me.'

'Not to me, it isn't!'

'Mum .. you see no wrong in me, but at times I've been a bad boy.'

I held on until after I left the prison, then I cried and cried. The media was killing him – and the rest of the family too. The boys got the news of Amy's affair from their friends, they read about how glad Mitch was that Blake was in prison. Janis Winehouse went on record saying how it was like a knife in her stomach when Blake said "hi mum" to her, she asked herself "who is this nothing, calling me mum?" As far as I was concerned, Janis Winehouse was nothing herself, without Amy. And, if it was like a knife in her stomach, now she and Mitch were sticking the knife into Blake and twisting it at every opportunity, blaming him for everything Amy did. Well, I thought, Blake didn't make her have an affair, that's for sure, she did that on her own. And I wondered to myself, would the media and Amy's family have cared so much if she was just an ordinary checkout girl in the local supermarket? I didn't think so. They loved the fame – and almost certainly the money too. Amy brought them both, and Blake was in the way. What they seemed to forget was, without Blake, the Back to Black record which made all the money and fame, would never had been made and Amy might have gone on as a little-known club singer with a great voice – like so many others.

The papers had a system which they called "cut and stitch" for stuff that had been used before and could be re-used. But not everything was cut and stitched. Every day there was something new from a "close source" of Amy's – a "close source" said this, or a "close source" said that. Although I believed I already knew who that "close source" was, I tried to get some evidence to prove it. I telephoned the papers. Some of them were friendly.

'Mitch is behind most of it, Georgette, he makes no secret of how he feels about Blake.'

'Why not say "Mitch said" then, instead of "a close source said"?'

'That's the way it is.'

And, I thought, if Mitch really wanted to "save Amy" then he'd be better off admitting to his own failures as a father, rather than blaming Blake every time the bloody cat had kittens. As long as Amy allowed Mitch to control her, I believed she'd never find peace, and Blake would never be safe near him.

Despite all this, despite the fact that my son was being kicked while he was down, and despite the fact that I was angry, and despite the fact that Amy's behaviour sometimes offended me, I never allowed myself to hate her – as I hated so many other people.

Then, one Monday, I arrived at Pentonville for my visit as usual at 1.50pm. I went through the ritual of the searching and the waiting and the degradation, as usual. I expected this time to be the same as all the other times. But, when I got to the visiting room, I was told Blake was "in the box".

'The box? What's the box?'

'Where you see Blake, in that glass box over there.'

I looked across at the glass box, it was horrible. I began to panic.

'Why?'

'I'm sorry, it's the rule.'

'What's he done? Please don't do this to me, I haven't done anything wrong.'

'Sorry. Please go to the box.'

I walked across to the glass box and went inside. I was so frightened. The prison officer locked me in.

'Please don't lock the door!'

'I have to.'

'What if there's a fire? You might forget me.'

'I won't.'

I'd been made to leave everything outside the box. I wasn't allowed to bring anything in with me. The smell of sweat and dirt was horrible – unbearable. My heart was pounding. I sat on a chair that couldn't be moved in my claustrophobic half of the small cubicle and wondered why this was happening. I looked through the grimy glass partition, into the equally claustrophobic section at the other side. I imagined all the other visitors were watching me, as the tears rolled down my face. I had nothing to wipe my eyes with, as I'd been made to leave my bag outside. How could I allow Blake to see me like this? Then I noticed a small tissue on the floor, I picked it up and dabbed my nose and eyes with it. I wondered how many other people had done the same thing, but I didn't care. I replaced the tissue on the floor and waited for Blake.

'I'm so sorry to have to see you in this box, mum. I promise I haven't had drugs.'

'Then, why are we here?'

'I don't know. Sometimes it's like that in here, you're guilty all the time.'

He looked so sad, so very unhappy.

'Mum .. Amy had the dog test, and the bloody dog sat down.'

'Oh my God! But, they let her in? Did she have anything on her?'

'Of course not, Amy wouldn't do that, mum.'

The dog test was when you had to go into a room and allow the drugs dog to go around you and smell for narcotics.

'It's going to be like this for at least six weeks, mum. I don't want you to visit me in this box again. I don't want to see you like this. Get Daydreams to do the visits until I get out of here.'

I knew he was right, I couldn't see him like this, I wasn't brave enough to come here and sit in the box every week. No mother should have to do such a thing. I didn't want to stop visiting either, but this wasn't a visit – this was a form of torture.

I called Kate Anderson when I got back home. I told her about the horrible closed visit and told her I was going to write to the Governor of

Pentonville. I wanted to know what Blake had done to deserve the box. I asked her if she knew about Amy's visit and the dog test. She said she did. She confirmed that the closed visits would last for six weeks and promised she'd write to the Governor too.

'The sad fact is, there are drugs in Pentonville, Georgette. It's part of prison life.'

I knew, of course, that it was part of prison life. Deep down in my heart, I knew I was paying for some of it, even if I didn't ask myself the question, what did that make me? But I wanted to know if Amy had taken drugs in with her. The dog was only supposed to sit if the person was carrying drugs. I wanted to know if that was why Blake was on closed visits and, if it was, why hadn't Amy been charged with anything. The Governor replied to the letters. He didn't really tell me much.

"Blake is on closed visits due to certain intelligence
  we have gathered. At first, the closed visits were
  restricted to his wife. But, regrettably, we have
  decided to extend them to the rest of his family".

That's all. What did it mean? Was Amy carrying drugs? Did Blake fail a drug test?

I'll probably never know.

Blake was also spending a lot of time in solitary confinement. He spoke to me about it on the phone, when he was allowed to call.

'Actually, I like it, mum. It keeps me focused.'

'Aren't you lonely?'

'Yes, a bit. I read a lot. Don't worry, mum, it's better for me than on the wing.'

I thought of him alone all day. It was horrible. Yet, when he spoke about it, I sensed he was safe. He felt safe.

'Sometimes, mum, I ask to be put in solitary.'

'Why would you do that?'

'I'm away from all the shit.'

I wondered what shit he was talking about and why anyone would want to be alone so much – solitary is twenty-three hours locked up alone, and one hour to exercise alone. Why would he choose that? Yet, he did. He seemed to spend more time in solitary and on closed visits than any other prisoner in Pentonville.

The media pack was baying again, in full cry. They found out about the closed visits and the solitary confinement and they loved it. The "junkie" was at it again. They didn't know, or didn't care, that the dog had sat for Amy. The closed visits lasted for the rest of Blake's stay in Pentonville, over three months, that's how long he was deprived of any outside contact, except for the visits Giles made to the box – and he hadn't even been convicted of a crime.

I didn't get to see him again until the trial.

How I hated Pentonville!

CHAPTER 10
TRIAL AND RETRIBUTION

Blake went to trial on 14th July 2008 at Snaresbrook Crown Court – he had already spent seven months on remand in Pentonville. Both the GBH and conspiracy charges were tried together, which was good for Blake, the lawyers said. It would be a difficult case to prove. James King himself, who was the victim in the GBH charge, was also charged with conspiracy, which made him a very unreliable witness. How could he be considered a victim, if he was also a perpetrator? It was almost a bad joke, but I wasn't laughing. Nothing was funny – nothing at all.

The trial started on a Monday. Alex Foden had telephoned the week before.

'Hi Georgette, I need to know Blake's shirt size. I've asked Amy, but you know how it is.'

I knew how it was. Alex wanted Blake to look and feel good and he agreed to take care of the clothes side of things. I'd been hostile to Alex at times and here he was now, ringing me to make sure Blake had proper clothes, because Amy was incapable of doing it. We sent Blake a suit and some shirts, via Kate Anderson's office. I bought some aftershave and gave it to Kate. I believed it would help Blake feel good in himself.

'I won't be able to leave it with him, Georgette. I'll have to bring it back.'

'That's OK, as long as you give it to him every morning, before he goes into court.'

It was very important to me that Blake should look and feel good. And Kate did do that, bless her, she gave him the aftershave every morning, for as long as the trial lasted. I don't know why it was so important to me, here was my son on trial for his freedom, and I was worried about aftershave. But small things become important in big situations. Minute, silly little aspects of life suddenly grow to huge proportions. It's as if you concentrate on the ordinary, to escape the consequences of the extraordinary.

Kate Anderson took me into a back room, when I arrived at the courthouse in Snaresbrook on Monday. Blake's barrister was there. They both told me not to worry, there was a more than good chance that Blake would be freed. He was pleading guilty and the judge might consider the seven months he'd spent in Pentonville to be punishment enough. I bargained with God again – let them be right and I'll – I'll – I'll –   God knew what I'd do, no need to spell it out. In the courtroom, there were two seats free, right at the front. They were for Amy and me. Amy wasn't there and I prayed she would show up, today of all days. The press gallery was full to capacity. I took my seat at the front. It was such a big courtroom and I felt so small. I wanted to cry again, but I knew I couldn't. Not there! Not in front of all those people! So I just waited, for whatever was going to happen.

Then they were brought up into the dock, Kelly, Kennedy, Brown – and Blake. James King was tried later, due to the fact that he was the victim in the GBH case. Blake looked so handsome in his suit, maybe a bit anxious as well, but so handsome I thought. We blew each other a kiss. He mouthed silently to me.

'Are you OK, mum?'

'Yes darling, I am. Are you?'

He nodded his head. When I looked more closely at him, he seemed to be a little euphoric. I put it down to relief – the case had come to trial at last and there was a good chance he could be freed. It couldn't possibly be due to drugs? I knew he was doing something in Pentonville – but not on the first day of trial! I went into denial mode again. I thought beforehand that I'd surely cry again, but I didn't. The tears were at the back of my eyes, lurking, but they didn't come. I don't know why. Maybe it was because I knew I had to be strong for my son, show a defiant and determined face to the world. Maybe it was for myself.

Blake had spoken to me before it all started.

'The worst case scenario is twenty-seven months, mum. With mitigation, I could be free by Friday.'

'That's what I'm praying for, my darling.'

But I was also worrying, if he was released, where would he go? Who would he go to? Me or Amy? If he went back to Amy, what would happen then? Would he kill himself or would someone else kill him? They were the options. It's easy to kill a drugged-up person and make it look like an accident. Nobody would care. And what would I do then, if Blake died? How could I leave him alone, wherever he went to in the next life – I'd have to follow him.

Or would he be set up again, only this time to go to prison for a much larger crime, for a much longer time, maybe even for the rest of his life – which would be crueller than killing him? Wouldn't it? I pleaded with God and my pleas must have confused Him – please set my son free – please don't! Please do! Please don't! I always only just wanted him to live and to have a good life – to have love and freedom, but I'd lost control of all that. All I could do now was watch and wait, hope and pray – for the right thing to happen.

I listened to the barristers making their opening addresses to the bench. Ours looked confident and so did the prosecution's. I wondered did any of them care about the human side of all this. Did they lose any sleep over what they were doing? Why should they? They got paid, win or lose. It was just a job to them, not a matter of torture and trauma, like it was to me. I could feel the eyes of the assembled press on me. But then I thought, they're just looking this way to see Amy when she arrives. If she arrives.

She didn't.

The trial began and a sense of impending doom came over me. Blake had pleaded guilty, but the prosecution still had to outline its case – and I'm not going to outline it again for them here. It's all a matter of record anyhow. But the words they were saying sounded ominous, damning, doom-laden, especially to someone who had no experience of the criminal justice system, or its arcane procedures. The defence team spent the day begging – pleading for clemency and making excuses, explaining the mitigating circumstances, saying it was all down to drugs and then condemning the drugs. Begging the judge for mercy. I thought, if this is the way to go, then maybe I should be begging the judge too. Surely he'd listen to a mother? Blake looked across at me and mouthed silent words again.

'Where's Amy?'

I shook my head. He looked both angry and sad at the same time. I was angry and sad too, questioning her love for him again. Why hadn't she turned up? I wondered if it was of her own free will, or if she'd been prevented from doing so. Maybe she'd been advised against getting involved, against being seen to be getting involved, in case some of the guilt rubbed off on her, in case she became contaminated by it – even though she was Blake's wife and it was only natural that a loving wife would want to be seen to be standing beside her husband in times of trial and tribulation.

Who knows?

Although Amy didn't turn up, there were many of the friends she and Blake had made in the courtroom, each one vying for more attention from the press than the other. One of those people was a young lady called Sophie. She made a big play for Blake, blowing kisses at him and posing for the press. It was reported that Sophie was his new girlfriend, even though that was completely untrue. I telephoned Sophie and warned her about her behaviour. I said she might think the whole thing was entertaining, but it wasn't a movie, my son was on trial for his freedom. I told her I would ask the court usher to have her removed if she continued.

'Sorry .. I am Blake's friend.'

'No, Sophie, friends don't behave like that. What if Amy does attend the court and sees you performing for the newspapers?'

'Amy won't turn up.'

'Whether she does or not, Blake is still her husband.'

Maybe Amy felt intimidated by the trial, maybe she was deterred by the other girls who turned up, they were all competing to be the one Blake loved most. But she wouldn't have been alone, I would have been there – by her side.

As I said, I won't go into the detail of the learned proceedings here, it's all on record and the papers have reported it in great detail, even if that detail wasn't always the complete truth. I felt responsible for not telling what I knew and, as the trial went on, my sense of guilt increased. I hated the feeling. I wondered if anyone else was feeling the same way – guilty for what was happening to Blake over there in the dock. But I knew the answer to that, nobody else felt guilty, nobody else believed they'd done anything wrong. Everything was Blake's own fault and he was just getting what he deserved. I'm not sure if Blake himself even felt any guilt, even though he'd pleaded guilty. I doubt very much if Amy did. No, it was just me, I was the real guilty party for not speaking up, for allowing my son to be manipulated again, like he was manipulated before. Sometimes I just wished I could die, there in the courtroom, listening to all the bluster and bollocks. I wished I would just have a heart attack and it would all be over quickly. I wouldn't know anything about it – ever again. The pain and guilt would be gone forever.

Then I thought, here I go again, death can't be the only solution. I mustn't start thinking of martyrdom, every time I feel I'm on my own in the world. It's pathetic! I have to be made of stronger stuff than that. Then I'd buck myself up for a while and the feeling would go away, only to return at night, when it could hide in the dark and speak to me from the shadows of my conscience.

If our children disappoint us sometimes, don't we also disappoint them on occasion? Isn't the making of mistakes a two-way street? Shouldn't we have more understanding of the world, of how things are – or are we just learning, like our children? Do we sometimes, in our mistaken convictions, make the additional mistake of giving them bad advice, or of setting the wrong example, or of not doing the right thing? We're all still learning, every day of our lives. The person we are today is not the person we'll be tomorrow. We wait to discover who we'll be in a year's time, or in ten year's time – as do our children. I'm a human being. I have all the failings of a human being, all the frailties, all the shortcomings, all the inconsistencies. While I'm rectifying one mistake, I'm making two more. That's how life is – I can't change it. If I could, I would. If I could have had Blake back again as a child, would things have turned out any differently the second time round? You see, to have had him back again as an innocent, out of that courtroom, I too would have had to be an innocent again – the innocent I was when I first met Lance Fielder. I would not have been the person I was then, I would not yet have learned from the mistakes I hadn't yet made in my life. So how could things have been any different?

The trial ended for the day and I went to stay with a friend of Blake's called Sarah-Jane. Ironically, this was the same young woman who had made the little balls for Blake to swallow, just before he went to Paris to be with Amy. But I didn't care. I just wanted to be close to what was going on. It was like a circus in that house, all his friends trying to be the most loved, just as they had been in the courtroom – the one who loved him most and the one most loved by him. They seemed like children to me, they didn't seem to have grasped the reality of the situation. It was all strange and weird and on a different plane to mine. But, I suppose, that's how that world is.

Next day, I came to court again. Kate Anderson and the barrister seemed to be pleased at the way things were going. I wasn't! The courtroom was an alien place and the trial was a threatening ritual. It was all grotesque to me, medieval and arcane. I went back to chambers with the legal team at the end of each day's court session. Kate had tried to telephone Amy on a number of occasions, but she got no reply.

'Perhaps she'll show up tomorrow.'

'Can't you do something, Georgette?'

'I can't make Amy be here, Kate.'

'It's upsetting Blake.'

'I know, but there's nothing I can do about it.'

So please don't talk about it – just get on with your job! Those are the words I wanted to shout at them, in my frustration, but that would have been rude of me. The barrister went on about it, saying it would be good for Blake if his wife was seen to be there, supporting him. But I couldn't wave a magic wand and make her appear.

Amy didn't show the next day either. Michael Brown's girlfriend came to me and offered to go round to Camden and see if she could get her to the courthouse.

'You're here for Michael, don't get involved with whoever's round there.'

'But, what about Blake?'

'I'm here for Blake!'

I was angry, what mother wouldn't be? I was resentful. My son was in the dock, fighting for his freedom and it seemed to the world as if his own wife didn't care what happened to him. So, why should anyone else?

Every day, the court was filled with press, they were like vultures, perched on their chairs, watching their prey, waiting for the time to move in for the kill. And every day their newspapers spewed out their vitriol to the world, every day more and more. They said that Amy was wasted and couldn't come to court. Others said she was drunk and aggressive and didn't care what happened to Blake. Some even said she was in bed with other men, while her husband was on trial. I knew Blake was reading all this, or was being told about it and I wanted to shout again.

"She's his wife! She's my daughter-in-law! He loves her enough to sacrifice his freedom for her!"

I wanted to stand up and scream at them that I had other children, who were suffering because of their words – words that were crucifying their brother. But they didn't care.

They felt no guilt.

Like me.

And my guilt took away the right to stand up and shout what I wanted to. You see, up to the time I decided to kill myself, I always believed I was human, with feelings and standards and morals. But, every time I opened my mouth, I seemed to be selling Blake and Amy short somehow – selling them, each time I shot my mouth off to the press. It wasn't intentional and often my words were twisted, but I'd become a rent-a-quote mother who could be bought and sold for a statement. So I said nothing. In any case, anything I said now would only be used to beat my son's wife and, in beating her, I'd be beating him.

I said nothing.

Then the press released a story that I'd sent a letter to the trial judge. Blake's barrister asked me if it was true, but I denied it. Some of it was true, however, I did write a letter, begging the judge to let Blake come home to us. If everyone else was doing it, why not me? I begged him, I thought he'd listen to me, like the fool I was. I thought it would be that easy, the judge was a reasonable person, surely, just tell him how much I loved my son and how this was all a big mistake and he'd listen to me. He would be bound to listen to me. I wrote that, if he released Blake to me, I'd change him, I was capable of changing him. I was barely capable of putting one foot in front of the other, but I would have promised anything. The barrister was angry.

'This could have a real impact on the trial, Georgette!'

'The trial is already lost!'

'No, it's not. It's all about Blake's sentence. He could be free by the end of the week.'

And pink pigs might fly. It's like, you know what's going to happen, but you still believe people when they tell you it isn't. You want to believe them. You need hope! So, the letter went back into my bag and I never sent it to the judge – and I watched and waited as my son's fate was decided by people who didn't even know him.

After the session in court ended for the day, I went back to chambers again with Kate and the barrister. Everyone was angry, including me.

'I can't go on. I'm turning prosecution witness tomorrow!'

'You can't do that, Georgette!'

'Why not?'

'Because it would be disastrous!'

'For who? I'm just as guilty as Blake .. and Amy. I won't let him stand alone. I won't!'

Kate tried to calm me, to make me see reason.

'We can't stop you, Georgette, but please consider the impact that would have on Blake. He would never forgive you. You are his mother, please think like a mother!'

I thought I was thinking like a mother – about the welfare of my son. Obviously not, in the opinion of the legal eagles. All I wanted to do was say we decided between us to do it, me, Blake and Amy. We decided to do it because we could do it and we believed nobody would get hurt. We decided to take the law into our own hands, because the law was an idiot and it was, more often than not, manipulated by vested interests and the people who organised and controlled it.

I paused, in my frantic summation of the situation. I thought about it again.

'Question you motives, Georgette. Why would a mother do that?'

I questioned my motives. What was there to be gained from what I wanted to do? Who would I hurt most? What would the outcome be? That's when I knew for certain that Blake would be going to prison.

I questioned my motives all night, I went over and over them in my mind. I didn't care if I was sent to prison, I just wanted justice for Blake. I was angry with Blake for putting me in this situation? Why did he have to get into a fight with James King? Why did he agree to pay him off? Why was he so bloody stupid? Then I remembered telling him as a boy, never to back down from anybody in an argument, if he thought he was in the right. I also remembered agreeing with him that a payoff would be the best thing for everybody. Who was being bloody stupid now? I didn't know what my motives were, so how could I question them? The guilt came back. I hated being a mother, I wished I'd never become one, I wished I didn't love my son the way I did. It was such a long night.

But it's no use wishing this or wishing that, wishing you'd done this or wishing you hadn't done that. What's done is done! You have to deal with the consequences and stop whinging about it. That's what I told myself. I told myself I was just being selfish, my life had been turned upside down by all this and I resented the inconvenience. I lit up a cigarette on the underground train. I knew it wasn't allowed, but I didn't care – what could they do about it?

Send me to prison?

All I wanted to do was tell the truth, but everywhere I went, I was met with the same resistance.

'Don't do it, Georgette. Blake will never forgive you!'

I was up against too many people advising, warning, threatening and asking me not to tell the truth. To me, the reason they didn't want me to tell the truth was simple – because it would have harmed Amy. If you're a "star", if you make money for people, you will be protected at all costs. Nothing else matters, just the public's perception of you, the people who pay money to see or hear you, the people who make you rich and famous – they must not be told the truth, under any circumstances. Amy was never one to care much what anybody thought about her, but the people around her did care. Blake was nothing, a nobody, so he could be sacrificed. Everybody already believed he was a loser and a junkie and a freeloader and a white slave-trader and a criminal of varying degrees, so what the fuck? They forgot that I loved him. To me he was the sun and the moon, a man who loved his wife and who was prepared to sacrifice his freedom for her, believing she loved him the same way. But sometimes, back then, I couldn't make up my mind whether or not Amy only loved herself and Blake meant nothing to her.

I'll tell you later what I think now.

Amy finally turned up in court on 18th January. Her natural hair was dyed blonde and she was a wreck, stoned out of her mind. I was worried in case this would affect Blake's sentence. The press were all over her and the judge didn't like all the disruption in the courtroom. Amy shouted to Blake.

'Love you, handsome!'

One of the barristers gave her a stern look and she shouted at him.

'I'm not talking to you, I'm talking to Blake!'

It made me smile. But, as soon as I got the chance, I took her back to the room that was being used by Blake's legal team. She was all over the place. It was all I could do to stop her falling off her chair. She wanted a cigarette and, although there was no smoking in the building, I broke the rules and lit one up for her. I held the cigarette, while she puffed on it, because I was afraid she'd set her hair or her clothes alight. Both legal teams came and sat with us and gave her a run-down on the trial, but she was lost and didn't really understand what was happening. My heart went out to her. I couldn't allow her to walk out alone to the waiting media, they just wanted an opportunity to humiliate her. So we sat there smoking and talking, with me holding her up. We wrote letters to Blake, which Kate agreed to deliver to him. And I could see again that Amy really did love him, despite everything, despite the confusion and the manipulation – and my doubts.

She wanted me to come home with her, but I couldn't.

'Why don't you come back with me, Amy?'

'No, momsie, Daydreams wouldn't like that .. we both have to be strong for our boy.'

But she wasn't strong. She was sad and alone, even though she was surrounded by people all the time. She was mixed up and misunderstood – even by me.

'Blake asked me to look after you, Amy.'

'I know, momsie. We'll look after each other, won't we?'

I didn't know how to look after her. I was losing Blake to the criminal justice system and I wasn't strong enough to help Amy. We sat there, for what seemed like ages. Then Kate said we had to go.

'Amy darling, listen, the press are out there, so hold on tight to me, OK?'

'OK, momsie.'

'Look straight ahead and keep your head high.'

'We'll do it for our sailor.'

I held her tight. I was so scared she'd fall over, the paparazzi would have loved that. Then off we went, with our heads held high. I did love her in my own way and I knew Blake loved her in his – I saw what he saw in her, when I was with her. It was only when she allowed herself to be manipulated by the forces around her that I changed my mind and doubted her – then, each time I saw her, I changed it back again.

Friday came and the trial ended. And, despite my anger and frustration, I felt very close to Amy on that last day. I thought about her, about why she hadn't come to the court, except on that one day when she was completely out of it. What prevented her from just turning up like a normal wife? Her addiction, or something else? I suppose I'll never know. I could have cried for her. I couldn't cry any more for Blake, but I could have cried for Amy. I could feel her vulnerability. Her loss was my loss and, in a strange way, I felt connected to her. I felt sure she loved Blake and I knew she must feel so sad and lonely sometimes, even confused – just like me. We were both lost in our own guilt and grief. At times like that, I really believed she did love Blake, as much as he loved her and, when all this was over, they would sort themselves out and be happy together. Would I be proven wrong? Would time make a liar out of me?

The court had rebuked Amy on several occasions, even when she wasn't there, because it was alleged the money to be used for the payoff was hers, but they said she wasn't directly involved in the conspiracy because she was attending an awards ceremony at the time – which was bullshit! But no evidence was produced by the prosecution to implicate her as a collaborator. Why? Because Blake kept his mouth shut – and so did I.

When the judge was summing up, everyone thought he said he was releasing Blake to a rehabilitation centre. The court was in uproar. All the reporters telephoned through to their editors that he was free. I thought so too, my son was free! But we'd all heard wrong, the sentence was twenty-seven months – there was no mitigation.

After the trial was over, I felt nothing really. I just wanted to go home. That was strange, because I hated home – it hated me! I hated myself! I just wanted some peace. I was still angry at the whole situation – the media, the judicial system, the record industry, the Winehouse family, the drug dealers, the people around me, the world the flesh and the bloody devil. I felt let down by people who should have known more than me. I'd believed what the legal team had told me, even thought I knew all along they were going to be wrong. I still had to have that spark of hope, that self-deception, and now even that was gone. They told me they'd appeal, but I knew that wouldn't do any good. I even blamed myself for not being more resolute.

'You've done all you could, Georgette, you've stood by Blake, you've shown your love and support. Your son knows that.'

'I should have followed my instincts, not just during the trial, but way back. I was a coward. I didn't have the courage to say what should have been said.'

'Nobody can blame you, Georgette.'

I could!

All along, I thought that miracles still happened – and then I found out that God wasn't listening to me.

Or maybe he was!

CHAPTER 11
EDMUNDS HILL

Kelly and Brown received lesser sentences than Blake and Kennedy was given community service. When James King did come to court, he was found not guilty of conspiracy, due to lack of evidence. The Stephen Moyes tapes were enough to convict Blake, who wasn't even there, but not enough to convict James King who was there. King claimed he was coerced into accepted the money, even though he wasn't. All the friends, who fought for centre stage during the proceedings, went on home, including Sophie. Not one of them even went to see Blake in prison – including Sophie. It was left to me to visit him every week, to stand by him, to fight for him, to cry for him – to die for him.

After the trial, Blake was sent to Edmunds Hill, a category C prison in Suffolk. I was glad, not because he was going back to prison, but because Edmunds Hill was closer to me and I was glad that Blake was at last away from Pentonville. Pentonville was evil – Pentonville had hurt us very badly. "Prison" is a very hostile word – like "junkie" and "loser", but every prisoner has or had a mother. Maybe that mother loved them or maybe she didn't, but they all came to prison from a mother. One thing all this was teaching me, was empathy – empathy with those who are condemned. I know it's not a popular sentiment, but I don't care. The experience of prison, even if you're not actually locked up there, changes your perspective on life. You begin to see the pain all around you in the world. You notice homeless people on the street for the first time, you understand the alcoholic in the corner of the bar, you see through the veil of discrimination round the drug-addict, you become Christian, even if you're not a Christian.

Once, round about this time, I passed a vagrant in a doorway. But I'd only gone a few steps when I decided to turn back. I spoke to the man and discovered that he was highly articulate and had an interesting viewpoint on his predicament. I gave him ten pounds and felt a kind of warmth inside for doing it. Listen, I'm no philanthropist nor am I a so-called do-gooder or bleeding heart, but I remembered all the times I needed help, when there was nobody to help me and, while ten pounds meant very little to me, it meant a great deal to the man in the doorway. I don't know if he bought booze or food with the money and it's not for me to pontificate on the merits of either. I saw it as just a spontaneous act of humanity, no-strings-attached – either for him or me. An act of fellowship with life's underbelly, something that was becoming more and more familiar to me.

The man was there again in the doorway the next day. I asked him where he lived and how much it would cost for him to go home. He told me and I gave him the money. He wasn't there the following day. I have no idea where he went.

Blake had taught me that empathy, when we'd been together for our short little two-hour visits. I remembered it when we were apart, but still together in our individual hells, fighting our individual demons – him his addiction, me my guilt – in our individual solitary confinement.

I sent Blake a telegram in Edmunds Hill prison.

"We're seeing you Sunday, darling. Can't wait.

Did you see the full moon the other night?

Not many more to go.

Love you loads,

Mum"

I was so excited, I hadn't been able to give him a hug for three months. I couldn't wait to get there. We pulled the directions from the internet and set off, Giles and I. We had plenty of time to begin with, so we stopped off somewhere and had lunch. It was a beautiful day, in more ways than one, and I felt good for a change. We got to our destination at 2.00pm but, to my dismay, it was the wrong prison. We'd come to a young offenders institution by mistake. Edmunds Hill was fifty miles away. I wanted to scream with annoyance, but I tried to remain calm. Giles was unflappable, as ever.

'Don't worry, Georgette, we'll make it.'

'I can't understand how this happened.'

'We should have double-checked the address.'

We had to get there by 3.00pm, if the system was the same as that at Pentonville. They don't let you in after 3.00pm. Giles sped through the Suffolk countryside, taking chances at intersections and roundabouts. Finally, we did make it, with minutes to spare. I ran to reception while Giles parked the car.

'I'm so sorry we're late. We got lost. Please let me see Blake!'

'Hang on, I'll see what I can do.'

My heart felt as if it was going to jump out of my mouth and run away ahead of me, into the prison to see my son. The officer at reception replaced the phone.

'Yes, you can go in.'

I could have kissed him.

'Thank you! Thank you! Giles .. we can see him!'

I was so grateful. I could see the relief on Giles's face as well. We'd be seeing Blake soon. Then the prison officer dropped a bombshell.

'Sorry, but he's on closed visits.'

'What? Why?'

'I'm not sure. Blake will tell you. Let's just get you over to him.'

I couldn't believe it. I'd waited over three months to be able to hug him, now they were preventing me again. Why was this happening?

Giles and I were put into a cubicle. We were separated by glass and there was only one phone between us. Then we waited. After a few minutes, I saw him – my darling boy. It had been so long. I cried, as usual. Blake was placed in the other side of the cubicle, with a partition between him and us. Giles took the phone and explained why we were late, while I tried to compose myself.

'Don't worry about it, Daydreams, you're here now.'

Giles passed the phone to me.

'Why are you still on closed visits, darling?'

'The bastards at Pentonville, mum, they sent over the punishment .. I still had a few more weeks in the box back there.'

'Can they do that?'

'Mum .. the bastards can do whatever they like. Give Kate a ring and try to sort it out.'

'I will. I promise.'

But I didn't hold out much hope. Despite the closed visit, Blake looked good, the best I'd seen him for some time. He seemed bright and happy.

'Michael Brown is coming here, mum.'

'That's good. You'll like that.'

'This is a better nick, far better than Pentonville. The officers are better, so are the inmates. You see, they're at the end of their time here, so there's no trouble. No bastard in here is interested in selling me, they just keep their heads down and do the time.'

We continued to talk for a few minutes, about everything we hadn't been able to say to each other since that horrible day in Pentonville. But I could see that the box was getting him down as much as me.

'Mum, do you mind if I go back to my cell? I can't bear to see you through this glass. It hurts too much.'

'Please don't go back yet, darling.'

'I have to, mum.'

He stood up. We touched hands through the partition and blew each other a kiss. Then he was gone. I wondered when it would all end.

I know what you're going to say – "prison isn't a holiday camp". It's an old cliché – "prisoners are there to be punished, not pampered". I know, I said it myself. But it's hard to listen to that kind of platitude from people who have no experience of what it's actually like. Let an ex-con say it to me and I'll take it on the chin, but not from armchair moralists or Sunday-morning pulpiteers or smug, snidey by-line journos.

I continued to send telegrams and I rang the prison often. That was one good thing about Edmunds Hill, I could ring the staff and they would tell me how he was doing. They were usually happy with his progress and they also told me he was helping other prisoners with reading and writing and even counselling. I always felt on a high when I heard things like that, whether they were true or not. It meant he wasn't taking any drugs and it was just heaven to be told something positive for a change.

I saw Blake again a few weeks later, this time on an open visit. It had been over four months since I was able to hug him and I was overwhelmed by the novelty of it. I couldn't stop kissing him. He looked

106

bright and happy and it seemed to me that, at least, this prison cared. They cared about Blake, they had some humanity. It wasn't all just a cold, heartless ritual to them. The next three months went as well as any three months in prison can be expected to go. It became a fact of life to me after a while. Something to be coped with and got through. I went on from week to week, performing the mechanics of working and visiting but, all the time, I was thinking about release – about when it would be all over at last. That thought seemed to consume me. I watched the calendar like a bored secretary watching the clock. Each day seemed like a month.

Then, in October 2008, Blake was due to be assessed for home detention curfew, or HDC as it's called, where a prisoner is allowed out on early release with a tag, when they've done about half their time and their behaviour has been good. Blake would have been in prison for about a year and he was entitled to be considered for this HDC. I kept ringing Edmunds Hill, to make sure all was well – that there were no complications. When I visited Blake again, he seemed nervous about it.

'I know I won't get the HDC, mum.'

'You will, of course.'

'No, it's me .. and who I'm married to.'

We never really spoke about Amy much any more, we both knew she was lost. Well, I did – and Blake didn't seem to want to say anything about her. She hadn't visited much while he was in Pentonville, so there was no chance of her visiting now that he was outside of London. She was still in the papers all the time, looking drunk and wasted, with this man or that man – at least, that's the image the press portrayed of her. There were still many "close sources" ready and willing to supply the tabloids with an endless supply of juicy rubbish.

The only good thing about it was, Edmunds Hill did seem to have a better support system than Pentonville. Blake seemed to me to be more in control there. It looked as if he was coming to terms with Amy, as if he was tired of fighting for her love. He was even able to laugh at the thought of his wife coming all the way to visit him there. Her absence seemed to have become accepted by him. I still couldn't make my mind up about her true feelings for him, but I was optimistic.

'She might, Blake, you don't know.'

'No, mum. The Ville is just up the road from Camden and she still didn't make it. No way will she come out here.'

I would see all the other visitors, some with their children, so excited to be seeing their husbands and dads. I watched them run and hug each other. I saw the new ones too – the uninitiated, like I was on that first day in Pentonville, alone, afraid, intimidated, standing out from the rest. That's when I thought most about Amy, when I wished she was there with me to support Blake. But it seemed he'd given up hope of that, way back in Pentonville. I thought then that I'd never forgive her, for making me do it all on my own, and my heart would sink. But then I'd hold my head up and join the queue with the rest of them. I had the two hours with him – her loss!

There was one time the media heard a rumour that Amy was coming to Edmunds Hill and the press surrounded the place. They were everywhere. But she didn't turn up, as usual. Without the drugs and the control, would Amy have behaved any differently? Of course she would! I was a witness to how much she loved Blake when they were together and I couldn't believe that love had just disappeared, evaporated, even though Amy was giving a good impression to everyone that it had. I wondered sometimes was it all just a charade. Did they have some understanding between them – some long-term plan? Did they communicate intuitively, without even seeing each other, as real lovers can? Did they know something I didn't? Only time would tell.

But, one thing I did know was that Amy would be a factor to be considered in Blake's application for HDC – and I had a bad feeling about it. But I couldn't tell him that, I had to stay focused and positive, to counteract his negativity. Too much had happened for something to go wrong now. Too many tears had flowed under the bridge of my emotions to allow any person or process to jeopardise this.

Friday was decision day for the probation service. Everything that could be done, had been done. I believed that, at six o'clock the following morning, my boy would be free at last, albeit on licence. I was very busy in the salon all day, but I still couldn't take my mind off it. I waited for the phone call – and waited. My nerves were on edge. I dreamt about picking him up from the prison, making plans, we'd be together again after so long. My boy was coming home. Home! Woohoo! The phone rang at about 5.00pm. it was Blake.

'Mum .. they've turned me down.'

'Oh God, no!'

'I'm sorry, mum. They say it's about you and Fred.'

'Please tell me it's not true, Blake. Please tell me you're coming home.'

'I love you, mum. Please don't make it any harder.'

I didn't know what to say to him. The phone line was silent as we both looked for words, searched for some sense in it. I was in shock, the world began to collapse around me. I started to cry, hysterically.

'Don't cry, mum, please.'

'Blake .. I promise you, I'll sort it out.'

'Mum, don't! I'll ring you in a few days. I told you the bastards wouldn't let me come home.'

'I love you, darling, I won't let this go.'

I couldn't work after that. Why hadn't the probation people rang me? Why had this happened? I'd said I wouldn't let it go, but I really didn't know what I could so about it. I was seething with frustration and anger. I telephoned probation, but they'd gone home for the weekend – of course they had! They'd gone home to their families and to their comfortable little crime-free lives. I hated them! I'd been calling them for days, trying to find out what the situation was, but they didn't even have the decency to respond to the messages I'd left. They didn't have the courage to tell me their decision, they let me hear it from my son. They had come to my house and sat on my chairs and drank my coffee, with their snooty, Middle-England noses stuck so high in the air they scratched the ceiling. They sat with me for over two hours and nodded their carefully coiffured heads – "yes Georgette and no Georgette and three bags fucking full Georgette", and all the time they'd already made their minds up. They thought they were better than us, Blake and I, they thought they had the right to make decisions which affected our lives in such a momentous way. But they were wrong – they may have had the power, but they didn't have the right! Why had they decided to keep my son away from me? The reasons they eventually gave were drug-related, even though Blake had never been convicted of a drug-related crime.

I telephoned the probation service again on Monday, but they still wouldn't talk to me. They gave me the run-around on the phone and then passed me over to some administrator. I lost my temper.

'Surely being a probation officer entails more than sitting in someone's house taking notes and nodding your head?'

'Of course it does, Mrs Civil.'

'You need to fully analyse the situation.'

'Of course you do, Mrs Civil.'

'You people are just a bunch of middle-class idiots.'

'I don't think so, Mrs Civil.'

'You haven't a clue about the real world.'

'That's unfair, Mrs Civil.'

'Don't talk to me about unfair, you sanctimonious arsehole!'

He hung up the telephone. They had formed an opinion of us, based upon what they read in the newspapers and what they had been told by people whose opinions were also based on tabloid fiction, not on actual fact. Their judgement was biased and coloured and they had used their powers to underpin that flawed judgement. We were paying the price for their prejudice.

The problem is, society is ruled by a bunch of self-righteous, hypocritical bigots who make up the rules – until the shit lands at their door. Then they conveniently change the rules, to suit their own circumstances. I wrote to the prison, but that didn't get me anywhere either. I contacted the legal people – no joy. I was getting nowhere fast, but I never stopped trying. Anger can sometimes keep you going, it can even take away the pain – for a short time. I still believed then that, if there was a light to be found, I would find it, whatever it took. How naive can you get?

Instead of allowing Blake home to me on HDC, probation came up with another idea. They suggested Blake should be sent to a hostel. How's that for bureaucratic imbecility? A hostel, that's full of people with problems, run by people on minimum wages, who are only too happy to sell stories to the press. A bloody hostel that would soon be identified by unscrupulous journalists and become a media circus ! How was that going to help Blake, or the other vulnerable people in that institution? The people at Edmunds Hill prison suggested a "treatment centre" in Surrey called Life Works, it treated its clients for all sorts of things – eating disorders, drinking problems, drug addiction. It was very expensive, but Amy agreed to pay the fees. I saw it as being marginally better than being in prison – Blake would be in the company of addicts and alcoholics. But it was better than being at risk from violence – or being in the box. So, in November 2008, Blake was sent to the treatment centre they called Life Works.

It would have been better if we'd sent him to hell!

CHAPTER 12
VILLAGE OF THE DAMNED

We had moved to Claypole, Lincolnshire, round about seven years previous to all the trouble, Giles and I – and the boys. Cromwell Cottage was a pretty house, with nice neighbours and a relaxed quietness about it, like a tranquil aura. It was, kind of, a new beginning for me – after Spain and Surrey and other places I'd been. The boys were happy and did well at school, I got on with my hairdressing business and Giles secured a good teaching position. We were just an average English family, living in an average English village. Everything went well for the first five years, it was probably the only time in my adult life that I felt really content and secure. But then things began to change, not even noticeably at first, but rather imperceptibly. Tiny, minute changes – feelings – intuitions – vibrations. The aura began to crack.

It began with a growing suspicion that Blake might be taking drugs, a suspicion which I refused to acknowledge and quickly put out of my head, making a variety of excuses for the things which caused me to be suspicious in the first place. But the misgivings were still there, lurking under the surface, even though I decided to ignore them. Then Blake went to London and met Amy and the changes became more apparent, the tiny fractures in my anaesthetic bubble. I began to feel noticeably unsettled and unhappy, but I didn't know why. I began to question my own destiny, my proximity to fate, if you can understand what I mean. I would walk round the house and feel a sense of dread. I would feel that some awful doom was just round the corner, waiting for the right time to strike at me. Waiting for its cue, its Ides-of-March.

Reports in the newspapers prompted people either to sympathetic smiles or contemptuous sneers – knowing nods of the heads, as I passed them by. Reporters and paparazzi began to invade the village. All kinds of people would stop outside our house and blatantly stare in through the windows, as if they were looking at a fairground attraction of some kind – a freak-show set up for their amusement. I stared back, of course, but that didn't deter them. They gathered in little groups, chatting and pointing – I sometimes expected them to put up deck-chairs and pup-tents and take out flasks of tea and home-made sandwiches, like the tennis fans waiting outside Wimbledon.

The hairdressing salon wasn't safe either. The press would camp outside and clients would book in for hair and beauty work, just to get some information that they could gossip about later to their friends – or sell to the tabloids. People would stop me in the street and tell me they'd read this or that piece of fiction in such-and-such a newspaper. They'd ask me if it was all true and I got very tired of telling them not to believe everything they read. But they did – believe everything they read! The more the newspapers printed, the stronger became the opinions they held. I'm sure if the press told them that the world was really flat and the sun was made of marmalade, they would have believed it. If it was in the News-of-the-World, then of course it must certainly be true!

It's strange – well, maybe not strange, but certainly disconcerting, how even friends can assume a pained, twisted expression as soon as Class A drugs are mentioned in a personal context. Perhaps I did it myself before all this happened, I don't know. But I hate it now! In between sharp intakes of breath and self-opinionated frowns, they would pontificate piously about aspects of drug-addiction they couldn't possibly know anything whatsoever about. People became experts on problems they've never encountered and on people they'd never met. Hypotheses and theories and conclusions and standpoints and positions and conjectures were offered freely to anyone who was prepared to listen.

Then Blake was arrested – and things got even worse! At first people said how sorry they were, then the press printed even more outrageous fiction than before and the mood changed. Pity was replaced by hatred. It's not clear to me whether they liked Amy and hated Blake, or whether they hated drugs and hated Blake, or whether they hated the truth and hated Blake, or whether they just wanted something to hate and Blake was convenient. In any event, they hated Blake and, in doing so, they also hated me!

Maybe I'm being too hard – people love to be self-righteous, they love a scapegoat, they love to gloat and point and say "there-but-for-the-grace-of-god". They did it to the Christians who were going into the arena in ancient Rome. They did at public executions in the dark and middle ages. They did it to the innocent women they burned as witches in the 17th century. They did it to Blake – they did it to me! Ignorance loves to triumph over enlightenment, hearsay over fact, opinion over erudition and lies over truth.

They chattered incessantly, like a multitude of noisy birds in the treetops, gabbling and babbling and prattling and tattling. In the corner shop and the pub and the butchers, the bakers, the candlestick makers! If I walked in, the conversation would stop and everyone would look at me. I kept my head high and smiled, of course, but inside I was dying – despite closing my ears, I could still hear their whispers.

'That's his mother ..'

'The junkie's.'

'The devil boy.'

'That's the devil boy's mother ..'

I told myself they knew nothing. They didn't know me, they didn't know Blake – so how could they know what they were talking about? I told myself that none of them could afford to throw stones – they were all thieves and adulterers and alcoholics and paedophiles and probably serial-killers as well. I told myself that nobody cared what they said or thought, particularly not me! But it didn't help, to tell myself that. It still hurt, all the spite and shite. I did care.

It's not as if Blake was the only drug-addict in the village. No, there were others – some had even attended rehab units. But they weren't destroying Amy Winehouse, were they? They weren't public enemy number one! Herod Antichrist! People would walk past my windows at night, shouting.

'Junkie!'

They knew I could hear them, they meant for me to hear them. I wanted to go out into the road and shout back at them.

'Fornicator! Alcoholic!'

I wanted to tell the newspapers all their dirty little secrets. Expose their dirty little affairs to the world, expose their addictions and predilections to anyone and everyone. I wanted to climb up onto the roof and scream it out to their wives and mothers and their whole holier-than-thou fucking families.

The kids at school would call Blake a junkie. If a particular lesson at school had something to do with drugs, my sons were always asked if they wanted to leave the room, if the lesson was too personal for them, if they would be alright – how embarrassing and condescending! The pressure on them was intense, constant, intolerable. And the police always seemed to be at my door. If there was a burglary, the local constabulary always came to me first. And they would always make some comment about Blake.

'Is this anything to do with your lad?'

'My boys are in bed.'

'No, the son that's always in the newspapers.'

Everybody had an opinion, and assumed that I wanted to hear their opinion. It would have been comical if it wasn't so heartbreaking. Sometimes I got sarcastic.

'Yes, Blake broke in to steal their daffodils. He likes to smoke them.'

And that's how it was, even when Blake was in prison. Once, when my neighbour had his house broken into, the police came and knocked on my door to ask questions – just out of pure habit. My neighbour had to shout over to them.

'It's my house that's been burgled, not Georgette's!'

That's how it was alright, over and over and over again. Whatever happened in the village, it was either Blake's fault, or Harry's fault, or Fred's fault, or my fault. I would listen to the drunks passing my house at night, shouting their filth at my windows, falling over. I would see the lechers leering at their neighbours wives. And the estate agents all said the village of Claypole was such a wonderful place to live – but they forgot to add, only if you're a behind-the-hand hypocrite. Only if you're good at finding other people's demons, instead of facing your own. Only if you like to throw the first stone, particularly at Georgette Civil. But stones have a way of rebounding and coming back at you with even greater force than that with which you threw them. The people who castigated Blake, who called him names – it could be their son next, their daughter. Sometimes I prayed it would, sometimes I wanted it to happen to them. I wanted them to feel my pain. I wanted to ask them what it felt like. I wanted to stand outside their windows and shout.

'Junkie! Junkie!'

But, even if it did happen to them, how would they know? What would they do about it? I didn't know, I did nothing about it. How would they be any different to me? Oh, I can hear their sanctimonious voices.

'We'd know, we'd sort it out'.

But, they wouldn't.

Then things began to get really nasty – I had four ornamental bantam hens and two cocks, beautiful pedigree birds. At night they were locked up in their coop and, during the day, they had the run of the garden. The cocks were a joy to behold, if they sensed danger, they would crow and chase the hens to safety. I found them so wonderful to watch – so uplifting, so natural. One morning, I let them out as usual. They scampered about, full of life, clucking and crowing – the noise of the countryside, where I lived. I had to go out for a while and, when I returned, I noticed that one of the hens was missing. I searched the garden, but couldn't see any sign of disturbance or trauma – no feathers or blood, to indicate the presence of a fox. I finally found the little hen when I went to the garage. Her head had been severed and she had been deliberately positioned for maximum effect. I never found her head. This was a deliberate act of cruelty and intimidation. Someone had broken into my garden and garage in a prejudiced attempt to cause alarm and anguish, to frighten us – maybe even to run us out of the village. I got rid of the rest of the birds, to save them from the same fate. In essence, I was forced to relinquish something colourful and sublime in my life, because of the mindless vindictiveness of my neighbours.

After that, an anonymous letter was sent to the governors of the school where Giles worked, insinuating that Giles was not fit to be teaching. Another letter was sent to a local newspaper, also unsigned, telling totally untrue stories about Fred and some of his friends. You see, we all had a price on our heads. Anyone who wanted to make a few pounds just had to telephone the newspapers with a story – it didn't matter whether or not it was true – and they could make themselves some easy money by dishing whatever dirt they decided to conjure up about us. Every day I saw Amy in the papers and every day I worried about who was going to blame us – who was going to get nasty with me or the boys on the street. We weren't giving her the drugs and the booze, we didn't ask her to appear in public the way she did, but we were getting blamed for it

I stopped going out through the village, stopped buying stuff at the corner shop, stopped drinking at the pub, became a prisoner in my own house.

Eventually, as I've said, Blake was due to be assessed for home detention curfew. I was so happy. Amy had to be considered first, as his wife. Should he be allowed back to her place in Camden, North London? The probation service people went round to the house to assess its suitability, to see if Blake would be safe from adverse influences there. But Amy didn't answer the door for some reason – maybe she wasn't home, maybe she didn't get their visit notification, maybe she wasn't allowed to answer the door. I don't know. Anyway, my house was next on their list. I was so excited, Blake was coming home, to me – even if it was only for as long as it was for. I had so many plans for him. I was going to buy him a car, teach him how to drive, take him to the salon, he could be with his brothers. It would be like old times again. I was on a high for days. The probation people were due – the house was cleaned from top to bottom, then it was cleaned from bottom to top. Blake's room was decorated, new bed, new TV, new everything. The lawn was mowed, the hedges trimmed. My baby was coming home!

Two female probation officers arrived and we agreed together that Blake would have two drug tests a week at their offices in Grantham. They wanted to know if Amy would be coming to visit and, if so, what were my plans for her with regard to drugs and the media. I assured them there would be no drugs and we were used to dealing with the media. They wanted to know how Harry and Fred would be, I said they'd be fine. They asked if I lived close to James King, I told them as far as I knew he lived in Derby, fifty miles away. They thought that parking might be a problem, we lived in a lane and media cars could sit in the road all day and block the traffic. I assured them there was never much traffic in the lane and the media would soon get bored and go somewhere else. It was getting surreal, the questions. Major offenders like murderers and abusers were allowed home to their families on HDC. My son wasn't a terrorist, a serial killer – he just made a mistake by getting involved in a bar brawl. That's all!

Nevertheless, the visit seemed to be going well – or so I thought. I asked them to be truthful with me and give me their honest opinion, would Blake be allowed to come home to me? They said yes. They also said, however, they had to have a multi-agency meeting first, before a final decision was made, because Blake was a MAPPA prisoner – which meant multi agency public protection arrangements would have to be made. Multi agency public protection arrangements? What? Blake wasn't al-Qaeda – he wasn't IRA – he wasn't Mafia or Cosa bloody Nostra! I was getting a bit agitated. They spent several hours with me and, by the end of the meeting, although I was mentally drained and physically exhausted, I believed I had answered all their questions and allayed all their fears and I couldn't see any possible reason why they should refuse my son's HDC application. Blake would be back home with me in a few days. My heart was singing.

Several days went by – nothing came from the probation service. Several more days. Nothing. I telephoned them, but could only get their recorded answering service. I left a message, but they didn't call me back. I rang again, left another message, they didn't ring back. I tried to contact them again and again, each time leaving a message – but no return call. The sense of doom came back over me, that feeling I had when the cracks began to appear in my aura. What was happening?

Then Blake called. It was late Friday afternoon, I was at work.

'Mum .. they said I can't come home.'

I went hysterical. My staff had to calm me down.

'Why not? Why not?'

'Don't know..'

'What does that mean, Blake?'

'It's just an excuse, mum. You know it's because of who I'm married to.'

'I'll sort this out Blake. I promise!'

'Don't try, mum. I knew they wouldn't. I'll send the report to you when I get it, you can give it to Kate.'

I was so angry and upset. I couldn't understand. I had no convictions for drugs, or anything else. I was just a mother who wanted her son home. Why didn't the probation service call me back? What was their reason for turning down the application? Did they do it just because they could? Did the media have something to do with it? I had to know. Over the next few days, I rang them again and again. I left message after message with their automated answering service. They never returned one of my calls, except for that one time when they gave me the run-around. I wrote to the prison, I contacted Blake's CARAT – counselling/assessment/referral/advice/throughcare – worker there. Nobody could understand why his HDC application had been turned down. He was a model prisoner. Nobody could find out what the reason was – not the prison, not Kate Anderson. Nobody. Eventually, I had to write to the Information Commissioner's Office and demand to see the report under the terms of the Data Protection Act. It took me a while to get it, but they had to let me have it in the end. I was shocked to read what was in it.

The probation service stated in their report that the media would be a problem in the small village. They felt that reporters would knock on doors, looking for stories, and disturb the residents. Another factor was our closeness to the A1. I don't know why that was a factor, but it was. My attitude was also mentioned – they said, or at least insinuated by not allowing Blake to stay with me, that I was not a fit mother!

The final, decision-making probation meeting was attended by eight people, including representatives of police and other interested social agencies, as well as the probation people. There was also direct input from a previous village meeting, held in the local hall by the residents of Claypole, Lincolnshire. I was not informed about this meeting, nor invited to attend. At that meeting, they decided they didn't want a "junkie" living in the village. It didn't seem to concern them if thieves and paedophiles lived amongst them, but my son was not wanted. They decided this in their god-fearing and holier-than-thou way. My son's fate rested on the whim of these narrow-minded fools and there was nothing

I could do about it. I asked myself who was at that meeting? My friends? Their wives? Husband? My neighbours? People who would smile and say "good morning" if I met them in the street tomorrow? I couldn't believe they felt so insecure – or was it simply their ignorance made them behave the way they did? Did it make them feel important, to have such control over my son's destiny? Whatever their reasons, they have to live with that maliciousness. They never asked themselves the questions "if it was me, how would I want people to behave?". My son had been destroyed, and now they wanted to destroy me. I was being judged for my son's supposed sins. I was the junkie's mother – I was in a box with nowhere to go, it was easy to throw stones at me – I was an easy target.

Their decision was relayed to the final multi-agency meeting with the probation service, which took full account of their wishes.

It's so easy to hate, isn't it?

CHAPTER 13
LIFE WORKS

Kate Anderson telephoned to tell me the treatment centre had been sorted out for Blake. I was worried that the probation service wouldn't approve the place and he'd have to stay in prison. But they agreed and it seemed like the next best option to coming home – at least he'd be out of prison. It still felt strange to me that all this emphasis was being placed on drugs, when Blake's conviction had nothing to do with drugs. I had come to terms with the fact that Blake and Amy had being doing a certain amount of Class A substances and that this had continued to some extent in Pentonville, but it wasn't as if he was a hard-core addict. Was it?

I wanted to know how long he would have to stay at this place in Surrey and I was told at least six weeks, maybe more. It would depend. Depend on what? How he behaves. I spoke to Kate.

'Will he be free after that?'

'Yes, I believe so.'

Giles didn't like it, he was sceptical about it all. But I was filled with hope. Blake rang me, he was also up-beat about it.

'At least I'll be out of here, mum.'

I planned to pick him up from Edmunds Hill and drive him down to Life Works. It would be great, we'd have a few hours together. But I was told I couldn't do that, he'd be sent directly by the prison. I couldn't understand, my son was free of prison, wasn't he? So why couldn't I take him to the rehab? Still, I let it go. I'd be able to go see him soon – there was some light at the end of the darkness.

Blake arrived safely at Life Works on 5th November 2008 and I telephoned to see if everything was going to plan.

'Everything's fine, Mrs Civil.'

'When can I come see him?'

'Not for at least a week. He has to settle in first.'

'Can I speak to him on the phone.'

'Not for at least a week. He has to ..'

'I know, settle in first.'

'That's right. We'll be in touch. We'll send you details of all our services.'

And they did. The place looked nice, it seemed as perfect as these places can be. And as long as Blake did the treatment, so he could eventually get out, then that's all that mattered. Life Works telephoned after only a few days.

'We're having trouble getting Amy to pay the fees.'

'How much do you need.'

'Thirty thousand pounds.'

'That's a lot.'

'Can you pay it?'

'What happens if I can't?'

I suspected that Mitch was behind this. Kate Anderson already had an agreement with Amy to pay the rehab fees. Life Works told me Mitch had been on the phone to them, but they wouldn't tell me what he said. This was a mess. If somebody didn't pay for the treatment, Blake would be sent back to prison. I didn't know what to do, I didn't have thirty thousand pounds in my pocket. I told Kate and she managed to contact Amy. Amy paid the money.

Thank you, Amy.

Life Works kept in touch, as promised. Blake was fine, he'd settled in comfortably and I would be allowed to visit him after two weeks. I was really looking forward to seeing him outside a prison environment. My elation was deflated a little, however, when I arrived at the treatment centre. Blake was fitted with an electronic tag, so he wouldn't run off. As well as that, he looked nervous, uncomfortable. That worried me. He wasn't at ease. Something wasn't right here. I was made welcome and everything – that wasn't the problem. The problem was intangible, elusive, it was just a feeling, a vibration. Alright, you don't expect a person in prison or rehab to be happy, but it was more than that. Blake was more than just unhappy. We had a coffee and went for a walk in the gardens. Everything looked lovely – but it just didn't feel right. We went back inside.

Then I saw the problem.

One poor girl was suffering from anorexia. She was having trouble with food and she was being forced to eat in front of everyone in the place. Blake was getting very upset about it. She was so thin, but she was also very beautiful.

'Look at that, mum. Poor girl. They do it all the time, it can't be right.'

The girl was crying. She was only a teenager and Blake put his arm round her. She smiled up at him, tears rolling down her face. Why were they doing that, in front of everybody?

'They think it helps, mum. She needs to eat, but not like this.'

I agreed, but who was I? Certainly not a qualified counsellor or a trained clinician. I wondered what they were making Blake do.

'Mum .. they have a family week.'

'What's that?'

'You can come spend a week with me.'

'That's great, darling!'

'You can't sleep here, you have to find a hotel.'

That was no problem, I'd find a hotel. A whole week? How incredible, maybe my first impressions were misguided. But I was still uneasy after I left. I couldn't get the sense of unhappiness that pervaded the place out of my mind, the sense of foreboding. It was the kind of feeling you can get in a place on a bright Summer's day, with the sun shining and the sky blue, but you still know there's a darkness there, at its heart.

After a few days, I was allowed to telephone Blake every night. He sounded good and my fears began to abate. He told me about the counselling he was getting and it all sounded positive, it sounded as if progress was being made. His words were very anti drugs and it seemed, for the first time, as if he was seeing Amy in a different light. He realised that it was bad for two drug users to be together, it was too dangerous. That's when we first spoke about divorce, Blake and I, it was strange how it began – he had telephoned me, sounding angry and upset.

'Mitch stopped Amy from visiting, mum. I've had enough of it.'

'Darling .. do you think it might be better to divorce her?'

He didn't say anything for a moment – I'd made the suggestion, I'd broken the ice, I'd said the unsayable. The media was still blaming him for everything and I believed it would be in his best interests to divorce Amy, even if she did still love him.

'Do you think so, mum?'

'Yes, I do. Sometimes loving someone isn't the answer to everything. You must love her enough to let her go .. and free yourself as well.'

'Don't say that, mum. I love her too much.'

'I know you do, but that love is killing you.'

He didn't want to agree with me. In his heart, he knew I was right, but he didn't want to do what had to be done. I believed it was the only answer. He couldn't go back to her, not after all that had happened. I was so worried about his future – and what about her reported affairs?

'It hurt like hell, mum .. to have the papers say your wife is cheating on you and all the prison inmates taking the piss .. to read what they said. It was too much for me.'

I wanted to be near him, to hold him. I took it to mean he was finally admitting he believed Amy did cheat on him – and I convinced him that, under the circumstances, divorce might be for the best.

'OK, sort me out a solicitor.'

People say they understand what this is like, or what that is like – but they don't really. I felt his pain, of course, but I couldn't know how it really felt. It wasn't me in there, with all the convicts sneering and sniggering behind their hands. I could close my eyes and try to imagine how it would feel, if it was me, but it was beyond imagination. You have to live it to feel it. But I was pleased he was coming to terms with his pain and that he was trying to find his own identity. It was a long and lonely journey, but he was walking tall now and, if he could do it, then maybe so could I.

'What about the family week, mum? Are you coming?'

'Of course I am, darling. Nothing could keep me away.'

'A whole week, mum. Then, on the last day, we're allowed out together for lunch.'

It's surprising how much small things mean to you, when you've been deprived of them for so long.

The people at Life Works did try to get Amy to come see him. She sent word that she would be coming down, but she never arrived.

'Mitch stopped her, mum. He really makes her feel guilty.'

But I was going to have a whole week with Blake, so I didn't give a damn about Mitch, or Amy either. I sorted out the salon, booked my hotel and waited to be off.

'Mum, you're coming?'

'Yes darling .. a whole week together.'

'It's only until 4.00pm. Will you be alright on your own after that?'

'Of course I will.'

'Mum .. you'll have to take part in the therapy.'

'What?'

'To talk about the Lance thing .. we need to sort it out.'

That took my breath away. The thought terrified me. What were we getting into here?

'Mum, I need to know what happened. You understand that, don't you?'

'Yes .. I do.'

'Was it in my head, mum .. or did it happen?'

'I don't know, darling.'

'We need to find out.'

Giles wasn't happy. He didn't like Life Works and didn't want me to spend a week there. He didn't want me to open my soul to them. I remembered how they treated that poor girl – would that be me? How would I feel at night, alone – after they'd finished with me?

'You can't really be going, Georgette?'

'Yes I am. Blake needs me .. and it might help me.'

'How can they help you?'

'I don't know. I just have to go. If Blake can deal with it, then I can too.'

'You're full of guilt, Georgette, that's your trouble. That guilt will kill you. Blake chose his own path, you didn't choose it for him.'

'No, but I may have helped put him on it.'

Giles was adamant that I shouldn't go, but he knew I would. I asked him to come with me, but he had to work. I could understand that. This wasn't his guilt trip, it was mine. I felt we were moving apart, Giles and I, I'd felt it for a while. He believed I didn't care what he said or thought, he believed his opinion didn't matter anymore. And, while that wasn't entirely true, it was certainly true to some extent.

A few nights before I went, one of the counsellors at Life Works rang. Giles took the call. I could hear his words, as he spoke to the person.

'How much are you saying he used? Are you sure? Yes, I will tell his mother.'

'What was that about, Giles?'

'Listen carefully to me, Georgette, the rehab have confirmed that Blake is an opiate user.'

'What's an opiate?'

'It's a drug, Georgette .. heroin.'

'So? Lots of people use drugs, it doesn't mean ..'

'Blake's a drug addict, Georgette.'

'No he's not! I know he uses drugs sometimes .. but he's not a drug addict!'

Giles sighed. The word "opiate" went round in my head. I knew Blake took drugs, I'd paid for some of them while he was in Pentonville. But, they were wrong, he wasn't dependant on drugs, he could take them or leave them. The old denial syndrome kicked into place again. I wasn't having that! I believed they all just wanted to spoil my time with my son.

'You need to accept it before you do this, Georgette.'

'Addicts can't live without drugs. Blake only uses on occasions.'

'He's a drug-addict .. accept it!'

'No!'

It was bad enough reading it in the papers, without Giles saying it as well. He didn't want me to go and this was his way of trying to stop me. Well, it wouldn't work. I'd sort everything out once I got down there.

I went down to Surrey on Sunday – it was 30th November 2008. I was due to attend the treatment centre the next day, Monday 1st December. I didn't sleep well that night. I wanted to sleep, I didn't want to be tired and stressed when I got there the following morning. But sleep wouldn't come, no matter how hard I tried. I told myself it was the anticipation of seeing Blake for a whole week, it was just excitement – but the word "opiate" kept going round in my head. It was a technical word, not an ugly word like "junkie" or "druggie", it had a different connotation – it was clinical, prognostic, symptomatic, definitive.

I didn't like it.

All night long, memories of Blake's childhood went through my mind. Did I do the right things, did I do the wrong things? Should I have married? Should I have re-married? I was so worried about what might come out when we talked about Lance. Did I stop Lance seeing Blake because I was jealous and insecure? Did I use my son to take revenge on his father? What would have happened if I'd done this, what would have happened if I'd done that? Question after question after question! And no answers. I questioned my motives, I questioned my conclusions, I questioned my recollection of events. How would I feel if my failings were exposed, if Blake said to me "mum, you let me down"? Would he list all the times I had let him down, let him go? Would I be able to deal with it? Would I be able to justify myself to him? I was scared. This wouldn't be about a child who had normal, average problems – it wouldn't be about him pinching a cigarette or a few pounds from my purse. It wouldn't be about him skipping college to spend time with a girlfriend. No, it would be about me – his mother, how I'd failed him, over and over again. Tomorrow would come and I'd finally have to face all the questions.

It's a fallacy – society's assumption that mothers automatically love their children more than fathers. It may be true in some cases, but certainly not in all. When I told myself my love for Blake was stronger than Lance's love or Giles' love, I was trying to justify myself, to exonerate all the mistakes I'd made, to make excuses for the shortcomings of my love – to gloss over my guilt. I didn't cause the hurt and disappointment deliberately. I didn't get up some morning and say to myself " I'm going to be a real bitch today". But I knew that, tomorrow, all the self-deception would be washed away and I'd finally have to own up to my failings as a mother. The so-called "super-mother" would be seen for what she really was – a pseudo-mother.

I prayed to God again. I tried to bargain again, but this time I had nothing to offer in return for my self-respect, except my shame. I asked

God to forgive me, to help me, to make everything be alright – I was really asking Blake to forgive me, to help me, to make our relationship survive what was to come. For the past two years, Blake and I had shared hell together and that word "opiate" was finally bringing me out of my denial. I was accepting that I had contributed to Blake's drug-taking, admitting that his oh so loving mother had helped to send him down the road to the place he was at right now. Tomorrow, I would have to take responsibility for that.

Morning came. I hadn't slept at all. I went down for breakfast at the hotel and sat alone, not really wanting to have to speak to anyone, to engage in small-talk and have to explain why I was there. The taxi would be arriving soon, to take me to Life Works. Part of me wanted to run back home, never to return, to bury my head in backslide, to be something other than what I really was. I wanted to go away somewhere where nobody knew who I was, where I would be unrecognisable, even to myself. Then I could open my mouth and scream and scream and scream, until my throat was bleeding and all the guilt came up out of me like bile and I spewed it out onto the unfamiliar ground. I didn't want Blake to say "I forgive you, mum". I didn't want that. I wanted Blake back as a child again, so I could do it right this time and he wouldn't have to say "I forgive you, mum". I wanted to be on my own with Blake again, without Giles and without Harry and without Fred – I wanted God to give me a second chance. Heroin, cocaine, guilt – they're all of the same genre. They all destroy. I would gladly have substituted heroin or cocaine for my guilt on that Monday morning in November 2008.

The taxi arrived and snapped me out of my delinquent mood. My humour changed on the way out to Life Works. I had a bad feeling, not the feeling of guilt I had before, but a feeling of foreboding. It was if I knew this visit was going to be short, and not because of anything to do with me. I rang the bell when I arrived and a porter let me in. I stood in the hallway alone, unsure, feeling vulnerable and still very uneasy. After a few minutes, Blake appeared on the long, open staircase. There was fear in his face.

'They're sending me back to prison, mum.'

'No!'

I screamed. A man appeared out of nowhere, he was a large man in his mid-forties, wearing a white shirt and tie. His name was Andrew (not real name) and he was someone big in Life Works. His face was angry, ugly. He shouted at Blake.

'Blake .. upstairs, now!'

I reached out to my son, but he couldn't come to me. He began to retreat back up the stairs, away from the ugly-faced man, who shouted at me.

'In there please, Mrs Civil.'

'Mum .. don't worry ..'

I was shoved into a room on the ground floor and the door was closed behind me, leaving the ugly-faced man on the outside. There were two other people in the room, a man and a woman. I stood there in a state of disordered bewilderment, looking at these two strangers. Nobody spoke for a moment or two, we just looked at each other. They seemed to be just as perplexed as I was. Eventually, the woman spoke.

'You're Blake's mum ..'

'Yes, I am. Did you know, they're sending Blake back to prison?'

'I'm sorry.'

'Our daughter is here. They break your heart, don't they?'

They were the parents of the young girl who was being force-fed just a couple of weeks before. I wanted to be sympathetic and polite, but my mind was in turmoil.

'I'm not letting them take him back to prison.'

'We understand.'

'I'm not, you know. Blake is not going back to prison.'

I shouted at the closed door.

'Did you hear, Blake?'

I was getting distressed.

'I'm going to get Blake. I'm going to get him, I'm not staying in here. I'm going for Blake and we're out of here. I'm not waiting .. I'm going to get him.'

I went to the door, but before I could open it, the ugly-faced man came into the room.

'This way, Mrs Civil.'

I was taken to another room on the ground floor. It was a horrible room, with many chairs arranged in a wide semi-circle and one chair in the middle – for the condemned. It scared me, the kind of scared I felt when I had to go to the dentists as a child. The ugly-faced man sat on one of the chairs and crossed his legs. I sat opposite him.

'I'm sorry, Mrs Civil, but Blake is going back to prison.'

He said it so matter-of-fact, like someone would say "how many sugars would you like in your tea?". His anger had abated now and there was no emotion is his voice, just indifference. I just stared at him. My eyes must have expressed my disbelief.

'What do you mean, back to prison?'

'We've called the police. They'll be here soon. You can stay, because you've been invited here. But you must not be near Blake when the police arrive. Do you understand?'

'No, I don't understand! Why are you sending him back?'

'He took a mood-changing drug.'

'What mood-changing drug?'

'Valium.'

'That's not a drug!'

'Yes it is. He went into drug-related behaviour.'

I knew Blake had had a wisdom tooth taken out. I reasoned that he must have been in pain. Valium is a pain-reliever, not a Class A drug.

'Yes, but he received it from another resident, rather than ask us. He has refused to give us the name of the resident. I'm sorry, he has broken the rules of probation, so he goes back to prison.'

I began to beg this man, beg for Blake. I began to plead with him, like I pleaded with God.

'Please don't do this. Please don't send him back to prison.'

'I'm sorry, but rules are rules.'

'But .. for three weeks now, you've given him something to live for .. some hope. Please don't take it away now.'

'Sorry, back to prison he goes!'

'I'm begging you for another chance. Please don't send my boy back.'

The more I begged, the more he threw my pleas back in my face. The more I cried, the more intransigent he became. I hated this man. I wanted to kill him. My anxiety turned to anger and my anger overflowed.

'You bastard! You self-righteous bastard! My son has a valium and you're sending him back to prison for it? He's just starting to come to terms with himself .. and you take it all away from him for a fucking valium!'

He said nothing, just sat there smugly looking at me, the hint of a smirk lurking across his ugly mouth. I saw the judge at Blake's trial, I saw the guards at Pentonville, I saw the probation officers. He looked at me as if to say "you can't win, you can't beat us". I wanted to jump up and punch him. But I didn't.

'If he gave you the name of the resident, would you give him another chance?'

'No. He's going back to prison .. and you can't wait in here.'

I was taken to another room on the ground floor. A female staff member came and sat with me, in case I became difficult. She had a sympathetic face.

'How are you, Mrs Civil?'

'I have a pain in my chest.'

'Should I call a doctor?'

'No .. do you think my son should be sent back to prison?'

'None of us do, except Andrew.'

'Then .. why let him destroy my son?'

'I don't make the rules.'

I heard a commotion outside, in the hall. The woman tried to stop me, but I opened the door and ran out. Blake was there, with the ugly-faced man. The ugly-faced man was holding him by the arm. My anger spilled over again.

'So, you're the bastard who makes the rules?

He looked at me, showing no emotion.

'Mrs Civil, you must stay away from Blake when the police arrive.'

'Neither you nor anybody else will keep me away from Blake!'

I seriously wanted to kill him, right at that moment, for his coldness, his lack of compassion. The feeling frightened me, I'd never been this angry before, or felt this level of hatred towards another human being.

Despite her empathy, the female staff member tried to restrain me. I screamed.

'What sort of a place is this? You take Amy's money, then throw my son out ..'

Blake broke away from the ugly-faced man. He rushed over to me. I held onto him.

'Mum, don't .. I'll be alright.'

'No, darling, you're not going back.'

'Blake, your mother can't be here when the police arrive.'

'Leave her alone. Just fuck off!'

The ugly-faced man left – angrily. He was obviously going to get reinforcements.

I had to act fast.

CHAPTER 14
BREAKOUT

The female staff member was visibly upset. I gave her a pleading look.

'Can we go somewhere, to be together .. before he gets back?'

She hesitated, looking round to see if any other member of staff was watching.

'Come with me.'

She took us to an office with a telephone at the very top of the building.

'Nobody here wants this, Mrs Civil, except Andrew. We all believe in Blake.'

'Can I call my husband?'

'Alright.'

I rang Giles and asked him if he could get down here straight away. He wanted to know why, but I told him there was no time for explanations, it was an emergency. The female staff member made us a coffee. I looked at Blake.

'Daydreams is on his way.'

'I couldn't give him the name of the person who gave me the valium, mum.'

'It's OK, darling. I understand.'

'I promise you, mum, it was only a valium. The pain in my mouth was intense. I did ask for painkillers, but I was just told to go to my room and rest.'

'They gave you nothing?'

'No, mum .. nothing at all.'

Downstairs in the treatment centre, we could hear the sound of the ugly-faced man and his security guards searching for us. The female staff member looked worried. Her job was on the line. I made it easy for her.

'Maybe we'd be better off in the garden?'

She smiled with relief, then took us down a back staircase and out into the spacious gardens that surrounded the place. There were many other residents and visitors strolling round, and we mingled with them until we could find a secluded corner. Some of the other clients were supportive of Blake because he wouldn't grass on the person who'd given him the valium and they made sure we weren't spotted, they kept themselves between us and the windows of the treatment centre. We found a seat behind some shrubs and bushes, with a view of the main gate. Blake was getting edgy. My plan was to run with him, I didn't know where to, I'd worry about that later. For now, we needed a car to get away from this place.

'Don't worry, darling, Daydreams will be here soon.'

'I hope so.'

We kept looking out from behind the bushes every time a car came in, not sure if Giles or the police would get there first.

'Mum, listen .. if the old bill get here before Daydreams, I can't let you see me being taken away. OK?'

'I'm not letting them take you. I won't!'

We waited. It seemed like forever. The other residents began to go in for lunch. Thank God for the tardiness of the police in Surrey. The female staff member came out into the garden to look for us, just as Giles' car came through the main gate.

'It's Daydreams. He made it!'

We ran to Giles. The female staff member came across to us.

'You must go back inside now, Mrs Civil.'

'We don't want to go back in, Giles. We just want to drive away from here .. now!'

'My passport's inside, mum .. and my money and stuff.'

'Forget about it, Blake, you can get another passport.'

'No, Georgette, Blake's right. We have to go inside. Don't worry, I'll sort it out.'

Giles followed the female staff member and we followed Giles. The ugly-faced man was waiting for us. His face looked even uglier than before – and angrier. A couple of security men grabbed Blake. Ugly-face barked out his orders.

'Blake, upstairs! Mr and Mrs Civil, this way!'

I held onto Blake's arm.

'Blake stays with us.'

The security men hesitated, looking at ugly-face. He nodded to them and they released Blake. We all went into a room on the ground floor. Giles asked ugly-face what he was playing at and ugly-face reiterated the charge of Blake having taken a mood-changing drug.

'What the hell is a mood-changing drug?'

'Valium, Mr Civil.'

'You're a rehabilitation unit, for Christ's sake! What is it here .. one strike and back to prison you go?'

'I'm not continuing this conversation with you, Mr Civil.'

'Why, because my mood's changed?'

The ugly-faced man wasn't amused and he walked towards the door. Giles' words followed him.

'Have probation been informed?'

'Yes, they have.'

'Where are they, then?'

There was no reply from the ugly-faced man. Giles went towards the door, where he was standing.

'So, technically, Blake is no longer under your charge?'

'Yes, that's right.'

'So, we can take him away from this place.'

'You'll be breaking the law.'

Giles had now positioned himself between the ugly-faced man and the door. I pushed Blake forward, whispering.

'Go get your things, darling.'

'Mum .. are you sure?'

'I'm sure. Quickly!'

The female staff member came into the room, just as Blake headed for the door. She guessed what was happening.

'Please think about this, Georgette.'

'I'm taking him.'

'Please, Blake .. is this what you want?'

'I don't know .. I'm confused ..'

Giles pushed Blake through the door.

'Go, get your stuff!'

The ugly-faced man tried to leave, to call his security guards again. Giles blocked his way.

'The police are on their way, Mr Civil.'

'We could wait here all night for the police to show up.'

I joined Giles at the door, blocking the exit from the ugly-faced man. The female staff member pleaded with us to see sense.

'I understand the way you feel, I really do ..'

'No, you don't!'

There was a commotion outside. Blake had returned with his belongings. The two security men were also there, but the rest of the residents had gathered and placed themselves between the guards and Blake. They were cheering Blake and carrying his bags towards the main doors. Giles and I followed, swept along by the crowd. The ugly-faced man tried to muster his two security guards, but they couldn't get near us through the throng of cheering residents – we could see him on his mobile to the police. Then we were outside and in the car. The residents were throwing Blake's bags into the boot and banging on the roof for us to take off. We sped through the gates and away down the street. The full implications of what we'd done began to dawn on me. I started to laugh. Blake laughed too, and Giles. We laughed and laughed, as we drove away from Life Works.

'Light me a cigarette please, mum.'

'One for me too, Georgette.'

We went to the hotel first, to collect my things. I looked round the room in which I'd spent such a guilt and grief ridden night. That was all gone now, I had other things on my mind. We crept downstairs, like real fugitives, so as not to alert the police, just in case they were searching for us. Then we left Surrey.

'Mum, I fancy a McDonalds.'

'OK, let's go.'

'I know a good one.'

'Where?'

'In London.'

The earlier adrenaline rush was leaving Giles. He was worried about what would happen to us. What would happen to Harry and Fred if we were all sent to prison. He decided to ring the probation service. For a change, they decided to be reasonable and said if Blake handed himself in to a police station before 7.00pm, he would just be sent back to prison and there would be no action taken against Giles or myself. Giles agreed.

We had the rest of the day to spend with Blake, so we headed for London. Blake showed us where he wanted to go. It was such fun, we took photos, went to McDonalds and then for a drink. It was so wonderful, I didn't want it to end. Then, before I knew what was happening, Blake's mood changed. We were driving through an area of north London.

'I'm scared of being sent back to prison, Mum. I hate being in a cell.'

'I understand, darling.'

'Mum .. I know a guy who lives down this street.'

'Shall we call him and get him to join us?'

'No, mum.'

I looked at Giles first, then back to Blake.

'Oh .. I understand.'

'Do you, mum?'

Giles was furious.

'No, Blake, we can't do this. Please don't ask.'

'Sorry, Daydreams.'

I stopped thinking straight then. My logic was all twisted up and I couldn't tell what was right and what was wrong any more. My son was in distress, he was going back to prison – for how long, none of us knew. If it eased his pain – if it helped him to cope right now, for even a short while, then why not? I'm not saying it was the right thing to do, I'm saying that it seemed to me like the right thing to do – at that particular time.

'How much do you need, Blake?'

'About three hundred pounds, mum.'

'Get it for him, Giles.'

'Are you crazy, Georgette?'

'If you don't, then I will.'

What was I to do? If I'd said no, how would he have coped? I wasn't thinking like someone thinks in an armchair in front of the television set. I had just broken my son out of rehab and I had to send him back to prison by seven o'clock than evening. He needed something and I could give it to him. What would you have done?

Giles mumbled to himself, as he left the car.

'For God's sake, Georgette ..'

We ignored him. Blake and I sat there in the car when he was gone. We looked at each other. The connection between us had fragmented, or else it was high on vagary.

'We could just run off .. while he's gone.'

'Shall we do that, mum?'

'We could, you know.'

'What about Daydreams?'

'Forget him. You're more important.'

' '

'We both let you down.'

'I'm so sorry for all this mess, mum.'

Giles came back with the money. He gave Blake three hundred pounds, then Blake was gone. Giles and I sat together in the car. We didn't speak much, just waited for Blake to come back. I looked at my husband and I felt I didn't really know this man. He looked so different than the man I did know, the man I married. I knew I loved him very much once, but now we were at an end. All I seemed to think about was Blake and all I seemed to care about was Blake. Giles knew it. He finally spoke.

'I'm worried about you. You can't go on like this.'

I knew I wouldn't be going on with him either. He was a wonderful man and a great father, but he couldn't cope with what was inside me. He had a girlfriend, I'd guessed that. It wasn't anything obvious, a woman knows these things, no matter how clever a man thinks he is at hiding it. It's an instinct, an intuitive feminine thing. We always know.

Then the gravity of what I'd just done struck me. I'd given money to Blake to buy drugs. What sort of a person was I? But the realisation only lasted a second or two. I dismissed it, put it out of my mind. I'd deal with it tomorrow or the next day. Right now, things were on the edge. Blake was late coming back. I rang him.

'Where are you?'

'I'll be back soon.'

I had to ring him again – and again. Giles was getting more and more irritated. We were late.

'He could do extra time for this. I hope you're happy.'

'I don't think I'll ever be happy again, Giles.'

'I should have known this would happen.'

'Why don't you just go, Giles. Leave me here.'

'I can't do that!'

'Then shut up and wait. We're late anyway, so it won't matter now.'

It was almost 7.30pm when Blake arrived back at the car. He looked terrible. His lips were swollen and his eyes were glazed. What had I done?

'I'm OK, mum.'

He wasn't OK. Neither was I. I'd just paid to put the devil behind my son's eyes and the devil looked out at me and laughed. God cried – after all I'd promised him.

'Let's just run away.'

'Shall we, mum?'

'Yes. Let's go.'

Giles intervened.

'Please don't let your mother do this Blake. She will if you ask her to.'

'If you don't like it, Giles, then go. Leave Blake to me.'

'Please tell her, Blake .. if she does this, she'll go to prison. And you'll do more time.'

'I'm not sending him back there, Giles!'

Blake saw sense. He saw, through the drug-induced state he was in, what I couldn't see. He saw the futility of it all.

'Daydreams is right, mum. I can't let you do this. We'd be caught in a few days.'

'I don't care. It's worth a few days.'

'No it's not. You wouldn't survive prison, mum.'

We were silent, all three of us. We were so late now that another hour wasn't going to matter – another two or three hours. I didn't really care anyway.

'Mum .. can I go see Amy?'

Giles couldn't believe what he was hearing. He turned and looked at Blake and there was anger in his eyes.

'I can't believe this, Blake. Why do you want to see her?'

'She's my wife .. I love her.'

He turned away from Giles and looked at me.

'Mum .. please.'

'Will it be safe?'

Blake rang Amy's management and made them promise there would be no police and no Mitch. They agreed. I told them I was worried, so they came on the phone and assured me that Blake would be safe and Amy would be so happy to see him.

'Please don't set him up.'

The guy on the other end of the phone said he knew some of Amy's people didn't like Blake or me, but he promised me it would be OK. Blake then rang Amy.

'Amy, I'm coming to see you.'

I could hear her scream of excitement. Giles was shaking his head in disapproval. We drove towards Camden, then Blake asked us to stop the car.

'Let me out here, I'll get a taxi. I promise you, I'll hand myself in.'

'Please do, Blake, or we'll all get arrested.'

'I will, Daydreams.'

I hugged him and he got out of the car.

'Mum .. drive off and don't look back.'

Like Lot's wife. But I did, and wasn't turned into a pillar of salt – I was already a pillar of fault. I watched him hail a taxi, as our car slowly drove down the street. I prayed that God would be with him, but I knew God wasn't listening – because of what I'd done.

The journey home to Lincolnshire was sad and silent. We were close to Peterborough when Harry rang.

'Dad .. the police are here in a riot van. They have the house surrounded. They want to know where Blake is.'

'Don't panic, Harry. Don't open the door.'

'What'll we do?'

'Where's Fred?'

'He's here with me.'

'OK, tell the police we're on our way home.'

'There's eight or nine of them all round the house. Where's Blake?'

'We'll explain later. Lock the doors and stay together.'

Giles put his foot on the accelerator. He was tut-tutting so much I thought he'd swallow his tongue.

'Now can you understand, Georgette .. if you'd run off with Blake, what chance would you have had?'

I wasn't listening. I was thinking, have the police nothing better to do? A riot van – my house surrounded – for what? Blake got into a fight on a Saturday night and then the man he hit got in touch with him and offered to sort it out for some money. Where was the sense in what was happening?

'You have to get your head round it, Georgette. Please try to accept that Blake is an addict, if not for me, then for your own sake.'

I still wasn't listening. I was worried about Harry and Fred – and Blake. I rang Amy's management, to see what was happening. They told me Blake had arrived and he and Amy were alone together. No Mitch. That was good to hear, at least.

'Is Amy OK?'

'Yes, she's happy to be with Blake.'

'Good.'

'We'll call you when Blake leaves. Don't worry, he'll be safe.'

There was no riot van there!

We arrived home about 11.00pm and there was no sign of any police. However, within minutes of us going inside the house, they came back, complete with riot van, and surrounded Cromwell Cottage again. About eight policemen approached the front door. They positioned themselves at strategic points in the garden. There were others round the back, no doubt. They could see through the windows that Blake's bags were on the floor. I refused to open the door.

'Is Blake in there?'

Giles went to the window.

141

'No. Blake is at a police station in London.'

'Can we come in?'

'No.'

'Sir, is Blake in there with you?

'I told you, Blake's not here. He's got a tag on his leg, for God's sake!'

The whole village was watching by now, all the neighbours out in their gardens or peering out from behind their curtains. Giles asked the officers if they had a problem communicating with the Metropolitan Police in London, or tracing Blake's tag, otherwise they'd know exactly where he was. But they still didn't believe us. They continued to stand in the garden, mooching round and looking in through the windows, as if they expected me to pull Blake out of his hat. Giles got angry.

'I can't believe it takes a riot van and eight or nine of you to come here on two occasions, to arrest someone who's in London. Will you please leave the property?'

'Sir, can we please come in?'

'No, you can't!'

It was after midnight when they eventually left. Someone with some sense must have realised they were wasting a lot of tax-payers money on a wild goose chase. But the damage was done. Tomorrow, the press would have a field day, trying to outdo each other with outraged platitudes. The village would be in full witch-hunt mode again, their Blake-meters going off all over the place – "Did you see the riot van at the Civil's?". "They were all arrested and Blake was murdering his mother and Harry was high on crack cocaine and Fred was found with a herd of stolen horses and the father is a head-teacher, did you know?" I could have written the script. It seemed to me then that we'd be hounded, condemned and crucified for the rest of our lives – all because Blake got into a fight on a Saturday night and then had the audacity to marry Amy Winehouse. Is this what our lives would be from now on?

I didn't sleep well that night. The word "opiate" came back to me and I remembered what I had done earlier. Next morning, after Giles and the boys went to school, I sat and thought about all the long months Blake had been away in prison. I began to talk out loud, to someone I imagined was in the room with me. The imaginary person asked me if I had any children.

'Yes, three.'

This person was female, I know that. She asked me to tell her about my children.

'Well .. Harry and Fred are teenagers. They're still at school. Blake is twenty-six ..'

She asked me about Blake. She asked me what he did. My heart was racing. My mouth went dry. I didn't want to tell her what Blake did, but a voice inside my head kept saying I had to. I began to cry.

'Blake does .. Blake is ..'

I couldn't get the words out. The imaginary person urged me to say them.

'Please .. no ..'

She told me I had to. She told me I knew I had to. I tried again.

'Blake is .. Blake is ..'

I paused, unable to speak for crying. The imaginary person was waiting.

'Blake is an addict!'

I said it again – louder.

'Blake is an addict!'

I continued to shout it out, louder and louder, until I was screaming. I screamed the word "addict" over and over and, when I looked, the imaginary person was gone. I was alone in the house.

I began to laugh. I laughed like I've never laughed before.

'Thank you. Thank you. Thank you.'

I needed to see myself saying the words. I ran to the bathroom and looked at myself in the mirror. My eyes were streaming with tears, from both crying and laughing.

'Blake is an addict!'

It was as if a weight had been lifted from my back and a door had been opened up inside my mind. I'd finally accepted that my darling son was a drug-addict. He didn't just use occasionally, or just when he was partying, or when he was sad and lost – he was dependant on heroin and cocaine. He had been dependant for a long time. The drug-demon had mocked me and laughed at me for a long time. But now I recognised it.

Would that help? Would the fact that I'd finally stopped fooling myself and come out of denial make any difference?

Only time would tell.

CHAPTER 15
PENTONVILLE REVISITED

Blake gave himself up to Bermondsey police station in south-east London in the early hours of Tuesday 2nd December. I was worried, thinking about him in the cells, he wasn't comfortable in small places and he might panic, even injure himself – especially if he was high on the drugs I'd paid for. I was worried if they were treating him alright, or if they were ill-treating him, because of who he was? I was worried if they had a doctor check him over? If they had, the doctor would know he'd been using – he'd know someone supplied him – he'd know it was me!

Blake was held overnight and sent back to Pentonville prison the following day.

During his first nine-month sojourn on remand in Pentonville, Blake had made a friend who he grew to admire and respect. The man's name was John Massey, he had been convicted of murder over thirty years earlier and had been sentenced to ninety-nine years in prison. John had protected Blake as much as he could from the other inmates – "muppets" he called them – who wanted to hurt Blake just because of who he was. John had helped him through the weeks in solitary and the pain of seeing Amy in the papers every day and not being able to do anything about it. John had phoned me from the prison many times, to re-assure me that he was taking care of Blake.

'Georgie girl, nobody will get near Blake with me here.'

'Is he alright?'

'He's OK. He'll be OK.'

'Has he everything he needs?'

'I'll make sure he has enough roll-ups.'

'Thank you, John.'

'No need to thank me.'

'Give him my love.'

'Don't you worry, Georgie girl, these muppets in here want to get near him because they know he likes a bit of charlie. But I'll sort them out, they're all a waste of space.'

John had his own problems, yet he helped Blake and, in helping Blake, he helped me. He gave me courage to carry on and to cope. His strength seemed to seep out through the prison walls and into me. He told me to ring his sister Jane or his niece Michelle, if things got too much for me – and I did. Those women helped me so much during that awful time. We would talk about when Blake and John were free, what we'd do to celebrate and how wonderful it would be. We'd run through Hyde Park, laughing and singing, we'd all get together in a big house and look out for one another, we'd be safe and happy and free. It was a dream, they gave me a dream to hold onto when things got really dark and menacing. John and his family became friends to me, more than any other people I've ever met. They were real friends, unconditional friends. They gave me a sense of reassurance that was both tangible and intangible at the same time and I'll never forget them for it. Blake would talk to me about John on the phone.

'Mum, he's like a father to me.'

'Is he, darling? That's good.'

'He tells me drugs are for idiots and he gives me strength to believe in myself. He keeps me fit, we go to the gym every day. I would have gone under without him, mum. He's better than all the counsellors in this nick put together. '

Now that Blake was back in Pentonville, John Massey rang me again, to let me know he'd arrived safely.

'I'll look after him, Georgie girl, don't you fret.'

'Thank you, John. Please give him my love.'

A few days later, John rang me again.

'Is Blake OK, John?'

'He's fine, Georgie. We think he'll be shipped back to Edmunds Hill. He's spoken to Amy. I believe he realises for the first time that he has to sort himself out.'

'What do you mean, John?'

'He told Amy, either she supports him this time, or he'll end it.'

End it? End what? I panicked. John could obviously sense the trepidation in my voice, even down the phone line.

'It's not what you think, Georgie, he meant he'll end the marriage.'

I knew this was true, we'd talked about it at Life Works. Blake so wanted Amy to visit him when he was in Pentonville and Edmunds Hill and later in Life Works. But he believed it wasn't Amy's fault that she hadn't turned up on so many occasions, he believed she had been prevented by her father and her father's associates.

'Amy was coming today, mum. She was on the phone to me .. then I heard Mitch in the background, he was telling her she couldn't see me. She was crying and shouting at him, but he just blocked the doorway so she couldn't leave. In the end, I said "forget it Amy". She was so upset, mum. '

At the time, Amy wasn't strong and Mitch seemed to be able to manipulate her. I believed she loved Blake and I knew he loved her, but something had to give. I'd planted the seed of divorce in Blake's mind when he was at Life Works and I knew he was resolved to go through with it, even though he didn't really want to. Amy didn't want the divorce either, but it had to be. They both had to find themselves to be able to begin again. They had to shake off the ugly past and wait for a time when the future would be clean and handsome. I knew they both wanted things to change, they both wanted the future to be free from vindictiveness and resentment. Amy would tell Blake how she hated it when her parents went to the press to slag him off.

'I'm so embarrassed about it, Blakie. I cringe at the thought of them saying what they do.'

Blake believed her – and so did I. I knew she wanted to get out from under their control and live her own life. And I know now that, although he needed me then, Blake wanted to get to the point where he could live his own life, and I could live mine.

But the defamation didn't stop, so the divorce had to start.

I relaxed a little, on the phone to John Massey, knowing it was the marriage Blake had talked to him about ending – not something else.

'Amy told him how much she loved him, Georgie, but Blake is different now.'

John's unsuspecting voice cut through me like a knife. He obviously didn't know what had happened the other night, how I'd given Blake money for drugs, and I didn't dare tell him. What would he have thought of me if I had? He would have thought that I was no better than the worst drug-pusher in Pentonville – supplying my own son!

'John, tell him I'll get him out. I'm going to hire another solicitor.'

'Will do, Georgie. But I've got my work cut out keeping the idiots away from him.'

I wondered who the "idiots" were, and if they had anything to do with Mitch Winehouse. But I knew, as long as John was there, Blake would be safe.

I was in the process of sorting out a solicitor to handle the divorce proceedings for Blake. I felt awful about it. I loved Amy and didn't want to hurt her. But, at the time, I couldn't see any future for Blake with her. Her family hated him and he would always be at risk with Mitch about. I did try one final time for reconciliation with Mitch Winehouse. I invited him to a private lunch meeting with me, to try to sort out the best way forward – how to come to terms with our failings as parents and how to best support our children. It was important to me, it matted that Blake knew he had my support whatever he did and Amy should have that support too. If Mitch and I could resolve our differences, then maybe the kids could sort out their problems. Sadly, Mitch didn't feel the same way and my invitation was declined.

Henri Brandman became Blake's divorce solicitor. It was the hardest thing Blake had ever done and there would be times to come when he would blame me for making him do it. But I believed, if Amy was truly the girl for him, then nothing would keep them apart, not even divorce. But, for now, I was just thinking about saving him. I wanted him back – the real Blake, not the drug-addict Blake. My dream for his future then was simply for him to be a part of normal society, to mow his lawn and fix his car on Sundays, to have lunch with his family, to go to work from Monday to Friday, to get married and love his children – normal, everyday things.

Amy went off to the island of St. Lucia in the Caribbean, round about Christmas time 2008. Blake tried to keep in touch with her.

'Amy's gone to get away from them all, mum. She's fed up with being told what to do and how to do it.'

Mitch was left in control of handling the divorce issue. Documents were supposedly signed by Amy, yet when Blake managed to speak to her, she was totally unaware of those documents (e-mail that confirms this). So, who was signing them? I believe that, most of this time, Amy didn't really know what was going on. Blake told me Mitch had phoned him, making threats about the divorce settlement, saying he was going to "get some heavies to sort things out".

'He wants me to sign a paper, saying I don't get a penny from Amy. I don't want her money, mum. I never have!'

'I know you don't, darling.'

'I married her because I loved her, I'll always love her, mum, you know that!'

Of course I did! And, of course, Mitch didn't get any heavies to sort anything out. He was just blowing off steam again, about money again – his favourite theme. I wasn't afraid of him anymore. Who did he think he was anyway? Some Mafia Don? He was getting what he wanted all along, wasn't he? So what was his problem? I had more important things on my mind – trying to support my son while he was in prison and doing everything I could to get him out. I didn't have time for Mitch's little games.

I tried to see Blake that second time he went to Pentonville, but I couldn't get a visit arranged. I believed it was a good thing that Amy wasn't around either – at least nobody would be putting money into surreptitious and suspect bank accounts. But that was really rich, coming from me – after all I'd done! The young girl with the eating disorder, who Blake had befriended at Life Works, was called Francesca. They'd formed a bond while he was there and he asked me if I'd bring her to see him in prison. We made contact by telephone and she was delighted to hear from me and couldn't wait to see him again. But, because I wasn't able to get anything arranged at Pentonville, we had to wait until he was transferred back to Edmunds Hill to make that visit.

After Life Works, my world fell apart again. Blake was back in prison and it looked as if he'd have to serve out the remainder of his sentence there. He still had fourteen months to go and, if he stayed in Pentonville, then he'd certainly be back on the drugs. He may have had some chance in Edmunds Hill, but the ideal thing would be to get him out of prison and back into rehab again, before something bad happened to him – a rehab that I would choose, not the prison nor the probation service. Prison wasn't the answer for Blake, he needed help and he wasn't going to get it in Pentonville. Life Works had failed, but I knew there must be other places he could go. Rehabilitation was the answer, somewhere that would give him a reason to live, a new purpose in life, somewhere that would make him believe in himself again and want to rejoin mainstream society once more. Hard-core drug addicts are people like everyone else, they have hearts and souls, just like you and me. They made a mistake in life, but who hasn't? Society, if it's a decent humane society, has a duty to help, to offer support, to try to understand – not to simply and blindly condemn.

Despite what had happened at Life Works, Blake also realised that rehab was his only chance. A little seed of renewal seemed to have been sown in him and it was up to the rest of us to see that it continued to grow. His habit needed to be turned round, and the way to do that was to make him feel valued and give him a sense of belonging. Surely that should be the objective of all penal establishments, not just incarceration and dehumanisation? I realised Blake's addiction was chronic, when I finally admitted it to myself. The amounts of class A drugs he was taking and the amounts of money he was spending on those drugs was obscene. It would be difficult to turn that round – but we had to try. These were the arguments that I put to the probation service. Somebody there must have had a soul, because the arguments and the pleading worked. Blake was offered one last chance.

He had to take it!

Before anything could be arranged, Blake was shipped back to Edmunds Hill prison in Suffolk, after only two and a half weeks at Pentonville. I was glad he was out of Pentonville, even though John Massey was there to look after him. I was glad he was away from the temptation and the danger, even though Edmunds Hill was a prison too and I knew there must also be temptation and danger there. It was coming up to Christmas and I began to reflect on everything that had happened since that fatal phone call from Amy, on 9th November the previous year. Was it just over thirteen months ago? I couldn't believe it – it seemed like centuries. So many hurts had been handed out and so much bullshit had been spoken about. The extraordinary relationship I had with my son had grown even more claustrophobic and the mutual love Amy and I had for each other had been brought to its knees. Giles and I had become like strangers to each other and my younger boys were being left unprotected.

I looked for blame, and I realised that was a futile thing to do. I had blamed everybody and everything, but it hadn't brought me any peace of mind. I examined my hatred, and I saw that it was self-defeating, it devoured all the hope inside me. I looked for guilt – and I found it, still lurking there in my soul. I thought I had been exorcised of it, but it hadn't left me – it just hid itself in my subconscious, knowing its time in the light would come again. I didn't know it then, but the guilt was morphing into something more dangerous, as it lay dormant at the back of my mind. It was changing into clinical depression, mutating into paranoia, shifting into psychosis.

I thought about the future. Where would we be thirteen more months from now? Would Blake still be in prison, or would he be killed by somebody he didn't even know, someone who would creep up on him when he wasn't looking? Would Giles and I still be together, or would I be alone with my unhappiness? Would Amy get herself sorted out in St. Lucia, or would she be dead from another drug overdose? Would Harry and Fred follow in Blake's footsteps and end up on the wrong side of the law? There were too many questions for me to try to answer, too many uncertainties. I needed some stability, some assurance of how things would turn out in the end. I needed to know what I'd be doing tomorrow, or next week, or next month – you know, like normal people do, when they plan for holidays and humdrum things and happiness.

But there was nothing like that on my horizon, I could see nothing like that in the immediate distance – only darkness and doubt. I think that's when I started talking to myself, instead of talking to God. At first it was only at night, when everyone else was asleep. I'd sit with a coffee and a

Baileys and ask myself the questions I couldn't answer. Then it was all the time, whenever I found myself alone. I wished I could follow Amy out to St. Lucia and lie in the sun and forget about everything – get drunk and lose myself in the alcohol. But that wasn't really the answer. My boys would still be here, all three of them, still at the mercy of life and its futile longings.

There had to be another way to freedom from it all!

CHAPTER 16
FRANCESCA AND THE PHOENIX

I finally got to see Blake at Edmunds Hill prison on Christmas Eve 2008. The visit went as well as could be expected, under the circumstances. I mean, what mother wants to visit her son in prison on Christmas Eve? Blake made light of it being the festive season, the season of goodwill to all men.

'Mum, I hope you don't mind, but I thought I'd spend Christmas with the boys at the club.'

It made me smile.

'Of course I don't mind, darling.'

But I did. How could I possibly enjoy Christmas, socialise and drink sherry and eat turkey and cake, knowing where my boy was. So, we made light of it all and pretended he was having a holiday with his friends.

Christmas Day came and went without much joy. I was glad when night fell and it was all over. Tomorrow would be another day in the life. 2009 would be a better year. It had to be. I'd hired a new criminal law solicitor called Michael Stephenson for Blake. It wasn't that I'd lost faith in Kate Anderson, but we needed a new approach. Blake had one more chance of getting out of prison and into rehab and I didn't want to blow it. I wanted to be in control of the process. Time was against me, I only had six weeks to put our case and sort out another rehab and, considering what had happened at Life Works, I knew it was going to be difficult. The probation service only sat at specific times in the month and the prison had an equally strict time schedule. It was very important that we should all be able to work closely together. Blake was pessimistic about it.

'I'll be the only one left doing the full sentence, mum.'

Kelly and Brown had already been released and Kennedy and King had never even been sent to prison.

'You have to trust me, Blake. I'll get you out, I promise.'

'Don't make promises you can't keep, mum.'

But I was feeling confident. Nothing was going to stop me, and I used this determination to offset the other weirdness that was going on inside my head.

'I'm not going to stop until you're free, darling.'

'Don't hold your breath, mum.'

He sounded so disconsolate, as if the fight had gone out of him. I knew he was preparing to divorce Amy and it was having a depressing affect on him, as if his world was coming to an end. But he didn't know that I'd finally come to terms with his addiction and, whatever about Amy, I wasn't ready to give up on his freedom.

Blake put Francesca, the girl from Life Works, on the visitors list at Edmunds Hill and she came with me to visit him there. She was only nineteen and so beautiful she took my breath away. She was still being treated at Life Works, but she seemed so grown up for her age, so mature, it was hard for me to understand why she had the problems she had. But we don't know, do we? We can never understand what another person is feeling. We might have a good idea, or be able to hazard a fair guess, but we can never know for certain. We hugged each other and it seemed as if we'd known each other for ever. She was nervous, she'd never been inside a prison before, but I kept her close to me and showed her the ropes. We booked in and produced our identity and went through the usual ritual of searches and were soon in the queue. She was so excited to be seeing Blake again and I knew he would be waiting to see her. It was a really nice visit. I knew they wanted to be alone so, after I'd chatted to him for a while, I stood up.

'I'll go now, darling. I'll see you in a few weeks.'

'Thanks, mum.'

'You have a nice time with Fran.'

I gave him a hug and went. I waited outside for Francesca and took her back to the station. We became the very best of friends from then on.

Francesca's family strongly disapproved of her seeing Blake, but she didn't care, she still came to the prison, against their wishes. What I loved about her was, she had her own problems and she didn't judge Blake for having his. I thought it was so beautiful that another person believed in Blake, like I did. But then Andrew, the man from Life Works, rang me out of the blue.

'Mrs Civil, we've had a complaint from Francesca's mother. She's concerned about your friendship with her daughter.'

'What's the problem?'

'She doesn't want her daughter associating with a drug-addict.'

'A drug-addict?'

'Yes, a drug-addict. That's what Blake is.'

I was furious. Who gave this man the right to telephone me in my own home and denigrate my son? Hadn't he done enough damage to us? I wondered what qualified him to be a counsellor of troubled people – certainly not his tolerance!

'How dare you speak to me like that!'

'If it continues, we will notify Social Services.'

'What the hell are you talking about?'

'Your relationship with this child is unnatural and we will have no alternative but to inform Social Services about it. Do you understand what I'm saying?'

I understood what he was saying alright, he was threatening me – and Blake. He was saying that he could make things difficult for Blake's last chance to get back into rehab – and I knew he'd do it. He had a score to settle. But I wasn't going to let him push me around, I'd had enough of being pushed around by petty minds.

'You do what you have to do. I make no apologies for my friendship with Francesca and I'm shocked at your shallow and insensitive attitude.'

I hung the phone up. And I was shocked. What was the matter with these people? Just who did they think they were? Francesca telephoned me some time later to apologise for her mother's behaviour. We decided to come to a compromise, Fran would continue to keep in touch with Blake by telephone, but she wouldn't come on visits with me again. I was so sad this had to happen. I didn't judge Fran and I couldn't understand why her mother had decided to judge Blake.

Nina, Michael Stephenson's assistant, said we'd need as much corroborating evidence as we could get, about what happened at Life Works, if we were to have any real chance of getting Blake out of prison and into rehab again – things like Blake's dental file to prove he'd had the wisdom tooth out, a statement from the person who gave him the valium, statements from the female staff member and from the other residents who supported him (available), we'd particularly need a new rehab that was willing to accept Blake – there was so much to be done! I got moving. I had the dental records within days and the statements were on their way. I contacted Blake's CARAT worker at Edmunds Hill, his name was Jonathan. We talked about a rehab centre.

'How do you feel about Blake going back to Life Works, Mrs Civil?'

'No way! Blake will never go back there.'

How could he even suggest that? Especially after Andrew's threat to destabilize the process if I didn't stop having contact with Francesca. It was inconceivable that Blake could be sent back there. What would happen to him then? What would they do to him? But, first of all, I had to make sure that all the paperwork for the probation service was prepared. I spoke to Nina every day, pestered her, pushed her, I don't know how she kept patience with me. I constantly rang Jonathan at the prison.

'We need another rehab, Jonathan.'

'That's my decision, Mrs Civil.'

'No, it's my decision, Jonathan. We need to find him somewhere new.'

'I think he should go back to Life Works.'

'You must be joking!'

'I know how you feel, but probation will require a safe unit. Life Works is safe.'

'How can you say that? It's not safe and it's not secure!'

I believed, if Blake went back to Life Works, he wouldn't come out of there alive. It was never going to happen! There had to be somewhere else, and it looked like I'd have to find it myself. Blake was prepared to accept anything, to get out of prison.

'We have to keep Life Works as an option, mum.'

'Those bastards sent you back here, Blake. They're not having you again.'

'But, if it means I'm out ..'

I wasn't listening. I knew there were other rehabs that were acceptable to probation. I did my research and, amongst all the places I looked at, I found Phoenix Futures. I called Jonathan at the prison.

'Yes, Mrs Civil, Phoenix are known to probation.'

'There's one in Sheffield, Jonathan.'

'Yes, but ..'

'We'll take it! How's Blake?'

'A little depressed, but he's OK.'

I knew why. I was worried about Blake's state of mind and what he might do, stuck in prison. I had to get him out, so I rang Phoenix on 9th January 2009, three days before the divorce papers were due to be served. They asked me all sorts of questions about his addiction and, for the first time, I was able to answer them without crying and denying. They eventually agreed to take him – on condition that he passed their assessment procedure. I was elated. I spoke to Jonathan at the prison again.

'I still think probation will favour Life Works, Georgette?'

'Sod Life Works! If Blake can get accepted for Sheffield, then probation will have to consider it. Anyway, who's going to pay for Life Works? Blake is divorcing Amy, so she won't. I can afford Sheffield.'

Jonathan was a bit angry with me for presuming to do his job for him, but I didn't care. Blake called me, he was so pleased.

'But Jonathan's upset, mum. He says it's up to him to sort the rehab out, not you.'

'And it's up to me to keep you away from Life Works!'

The Phoenix made contact with the CARAT worker at the prison and also the probation service, and Blake's placement there was confirmed, dependant on assessment. I relaxed a bit, everything was going to plan. My boy would be out soon. I still didn't let up, however, I continued to pester Nina with phone calls, she must have dreaded the sound of my voice – "Are all the details tied up? Have you written to Sheffield? Have you done this? Have you done that? Have you got the paperwork in place? We only have one chance, Nina, don't let me down." It was all sorted. It was up to Blake now. He had his assessment, scheduled for the

29th January.

In the meantime, on 12th January 2009, Blake's solicitors served divorce papers on Amy, based on a claim of adultery. How hard must that have been for him to do? He still loved her and he gave her her freedom for the second time. News of the divorce hit the media and they still called him a "jailbird" and a "druggie". They only wanted to report the dirt – the sex and drugs and affairs, not the pain and misery. I thought divorcing Amy and going public would somehow help. It didn't. Amy didn't contest the divorce. Her family had followed her over to St. Lucia and they were doing some sort of documentary over there, blaming Blake again, while he languished in prison. She'd been photographed with other men and was quoted as saying she was in love again and didn't need drugs. I smiled when I read that. She said her whole marriage was based on doing drugs and that, for the time being, she'd forgotten she was even married.

I rang Jonathan, Blake's CARAT worker at Edmunds Hill prison, on the day of Blake's assessment.

'Is Blake OK? Is he focused?'

'Yes, he's ready.'

'Can I speak to him when it's over?'

'Yes, I'll get him to call you.'

Then I rang the Phoenix rehab in Sheffield.

'Is everything ready for today?'

'Yes, don't worry.'

I had haunted all these people, morning and night. I had stalked them daily. I had to get Blake out of prison. This was his last and only chance and I wasn't prepared to allow anything to jeopardise it. But it was out of my hands now, it was down to Blake himself. I could only sit and wait.

The assessment went well. The people at the prison were pleased and so were the people at the Phoenix. I managed to get a call through to Blake.

'You clever boy. See, I told you it would be OK.'

'I'll believe that when I'm out of here, mum.'

'They said I can collect you and take you to Sheffield myself, how fabulous is that!'

'It's me you're talking to, mum. You know my luck, something is bound to happen.'

I was so excited. I rang Sheffield and everything was arranged for Blake to come there. I paid the fees, the prison was ready to release him – then the probation service said no. I couldn't believe it. Apparently, the Phoenix at Sheffield had omitted the words "immediate placement available" from the documentation, so the probation service refused to sanction it. I went crazy. I called the solicitors.

'What the hell do they mean, Nina?'

'They need the word "immediate" to be included on the documents.'

'It's just a bloody technicality!'

'You know what probation are like, Georgette.'

I was so angry, with myself for not making sure the documentation was idiot-proof and with the probation jobsworths for being so bloody pedantic. Something had to be done – quickly!

'What do we need to do, Nina?'

'Get the Phoenix to add the word "immediate" to the placement document, then arrange a new probation meeting.'

'But, that could take another month. I'm not prepared to wait that long, Nina. I'll contact the Phoenix and you get another probation meeting as soon as possible.'

'I'll try, Georgette.'

Blake rang.

'See, mum, I told you.'

'I'm on the case, darling.'

'It'll take at least another month. I might as well stay here until February 2010, then my full sentence will be served and the bastards will have to let me out."

I rang Blake's CARAT worker at Edmunds Hill.

'Please try to calm him ..'

I was frantic. I sorted out the wording out with The Phoenix in Sheffield and Nina got on to probation. We all prayed that they'd reconsider now, not in a month or two months. Nina called me.

'Good news, Georgette, Blake will be released on 25th February.'

I thought I was hearing things for a minute. Something had gone right for a change. Was God listening to me again? Thank you Lord!

'Thank you, Nina. Thank you, thank you.'

I called Blake immediately.

'You're going to be free, my darling. I'm coming for you.'

'I know, mum. I've just been told.'

It was the happiest day of my life, and it was the saddest day of my life. My boy would be free, albeit in rehab. But this was also his chance to be free of the drugs. It would be a journey for both of us and it wouldn't be easy. It would be difficult and painful, with times of anger and sadness, as well as times of defiance and triumph. Dark corners in both our psyches would have to be explored and neither of us knew what lay ahead, or how the journey would end. But we were ready to begin.

The Phoenix would be the first step on the road.

I must have been difficult to live with, during this time, I know that – impossible to live with, even. My mind was occupied with Blake every minute of every day, to the extent that I quite forgot I had a husband and two other sons. Maybe it wasn't so bad for the boys, only they can say, but it was certainly extremely difficult for Giles. Our relationship was already in trouble and this tore us apart completely. I blame myself now – I can see now how isolated and expendable he must have felt. I knew things were bad between us, it wasn't as if I was oblivious to what was happening. I knew it, I admitted it to myself, but I couldn't do anything about it. I didn't want to do anything about it. Giles believed I was consumed with Blake. And I was.

'If Blake says jump, you ask how high, Georgette!'

At the time, I might have fooled myself into assuming he was jealous of Blake, but I know now he was genuinely concerned about me. I was beginning to show the signs of paranoia, of becoming detached from the rest of the world – from reality.

'Blake needs me, Giles. How would you feel if you were a drug-addict in prison?'

'Don't forget, you have two other sons. They need you too.'

'I've never neglected the boys, in favour of Blake.'

'You can't live his life for him, Georgette. You have to think of your own life.'

That made me angry. He wants me to turn my back on my child, I thought – what mother would do that? Not me! Not me! Certainly not me! But Giles was right, as he was right in most things, I was consumed – but not only with Blake, I was also consumed with my own image as a mother.

I thought about Blake every day. If the sun shone, I'd cry because he wasn't feeling its heat. If it rained, I'd cry because he couldn't watch it falling on the leaves, like he used to do when he was young. I would send telegrams late at night, just so I could feel closer to him, knowing it would get to him the following day. Nobody sent telegrams to prison – except me. And that's how it was, and yes, I know I neglected the other boys – and Giles. It was then that I began to see a further change in my husband. I tried to ignore it and hoped it would go away, but it didn't. I'd known for some time that he'd found someone else, someone who wouldn't neglect him. I believed at first that it was just a fling, that it would blow over. At any other time I would have fought her, I would have taken her on. But I didn't have any fight left in me, it had all been used up. We had come so far and now he was leaving, before we'd reached the end. He was leaving, when we needed him most – me and the boys, especially the boys. He blamed the situation

'I can't go on anymore, Georgette. It'll never end.'

'We're so near the end, Giles ..'

'What happens if it all starts over again?'

'Then we'll deal with it all over again, that's what parents do.'

'I can't.'

I don't blame Giles anymore. I did then, but I don't now. It was the situation, and the village, and the school governors where he worked, and the woman he met, and me – and him. It wasn't just Blake. But I became very worried that it would harm Blake's recovery in some way and damage the boys, they couldn't take much more. I lay in bed and thought about it – how could it be. Only a few days earlier, we were planning a holiday for when Blake was eventually freed. But now I was going to be on my own – really on my own. It seemed like, every time I began to see a little light in the distant sky, the clouds closed in again and the darkness returned.

Would it always be like this? Would the pain never end?
Giles left on 20th February, 2009.
I thought about suicide.

CHAPTER 17
REDEMPTION

Giles did come back to drive me across to Edmunds Hill on 25th February 2009, five days after he left me. I had to pick Blake up from the prison and take him to the Phoenix Futures Rehab Centre in Sheffield. Blake was quoted in the papers as saying he wanted to continue with the divorce proceedings, in order to give himself the best chance of a drug-free fresh start. I was happy for him. I'd spoken to him on the phone.

'Don't forget to bring my hat, mum.'

'Of course I won't forget, darling.'

At times, when I was alone at home, I would hold his hat – the hat everybody saw him wearing in those pictures in the newspapers. I could sense him through it – feel him close to me. Now I held it again as I stood outside the gates with the swarming press pack – but I didn't even notice them, I was just another mother waiting for her son. We'd arrived at nine o'clock in the morning. I was so excited, full of anticipation, looking so forward to seeing my beautiful boy. I'd hug him to death – never let him go again.

I could hear the sound of metal doors slamming inside the prison. I knew he was on his way. I shouted.

'Blake's coming!'

Francesca had come along as well, against her mother's wishes, and Fred. They were standing with Giles. But Giles was being surly and wouldn't speak to either of them. The press reported that Francesca was Sophie, the young woman who'd made such a play for Blake at the trial, but they'd got it wrong again. I would never have allowed Sophie to be there, simply because Amy hated her – that was a good enough reason for me. Whatever I thought about Amy during this time, I would never have encouraged anyone she hated to come close to Blake.

Then I could see him through the railings. He smiled – a huge smile. I cried with relief.

'Hi, darling!'

'Hi, mum.'

Before I knew it, I was hugging him so tight I thought I'd crush him. I put his hat on his head and he hugged Francesca and shook hands with Giles, before we went off towards the car, through the press scrum. He looked so good, so healthy. I felt, somehow, that maybe this was his time at last, the time when he would be able to beat his demons and his drug-addiction. But whatever happened, for now at least, I had a small part of my Blake back. I might even be able to shake off the darkness and depression in my own heart.

We had lunch and talked incessantly and I wanted time to stop, to stand still. I didn't want to have to leave him, or for him to have to leave me. I wanted to be with him forever, for the past year and a half to have been nothing but a bad dream that I'd just woken from. But I knew it wasn't a dream, it was real enough – and it wasn't completely over yet. But, right then, he looked strong and I was weak from it all and, for the first time in this whole bloody saga, I found myself needing to lean on Blake, rather than needing him to lean on me. I felt a powerful desire to siphon some of his strength from him, but how could I do that without exposing my vulnerability and causing him more worry at a time when he needed stability rather than strife? Blake knew Giles had left me and I could feel the tension between them, the unspoken estrangement, but we all pretended things were normal and I was determined that nothing was going to spoil this time for me.

When we eventually got to the Phoenix Rehab Centre in Sheffield, we were allowed a little more time with Blake, to have coffee and get a feel for the place. It looked lovely to me, after all the time in Edmunds Hill and Pentonville prisons. But then, Life Works looked lovely too – on the outside. So I was a bit suspicious. Nevertheless, the people there seemed kind, until they told me I had to go. I didn't want to go, I wanted to stay for just a few minutes more. But I couldn't. It was like the first day I took him to school, I wanted to stay then too – but they wouldn't let me.

'He'll be alright, Mrs Civil.'

'I know .. I know he's in the best place. Can I ring him tomorrow?'

'No, sorry. You have to let him settle, at least for a few weeks.'

'I can't even ring him?'

'No, but you can ring the office, to see how things are.'

I started to get frightened. Was it going to be Life Works all over again? If I wasn't even allowed to ring him, when would I get to see him again? Why did these places have to have these ridiculous rules? Were they doing it out of pure vindictiveness? Did they hate me, like the press and the village people?

They gave me a passwords, for security, to make sure it was me when I telephoned and not the newspapers. Then I was hugging him again, as if it was going to be for the very last time.

'I'll be OK, mum.'

'You work really hard, darling.'

'I will. Promise me you'll be OK.'

'I promise.'

'Tell the boys I love them.'

'I will. I love you .. don't forget the moon.'

'We own that moon, mum.'

And we did. There were only six full ones left, until he'd be released on licence.

'Don't forget it, mum. They can't keep me inside forever. Six moons is nothing, compared to what we've been through.'

So I let him go – again. He had to recover, I knew that. He had to get himself back, it was his only chance. He'd been through the mill in prison and even before that, there was no point in being selfish and wanting what I wanted. I had to want what Blake needed. I had to put his welfare before my need. I'd promised him we'd never be separated again, all those years ago, and I hadn't kept my word. Many things had separated us since then – many bad things. But now it was time for us to be separated by destiny, by necessity, by divine proscription – or whatever the hell it was.

Blake still kept in touch with Amy, while he was at the Phoenix and she was in St. Lucia. He was getting stronger and was better able to deal with all the previous hurt and humiliation. I saw how he reacted every time her name was mentioned and sometimes it seemed to me, back then, that when he was free – I mean really free – he and Amy would get come together again.

'Shall I write your script for you, darling?'

'Go on then, mum.'

'In February, I think you will join Amy, wherever she is.'

'What makes you think that?'

'Because I know you, Blake.'

'Clever mum.'

Francesca continued to come with me when I visited Blake at Sheffield. We'd meet at the station and go up to the rehab together. She loved Blake and Blake loved her – they were so good together. But my own life was growing darker at this time, for some reason – I can't explain why. Something had gotten inside me and I didn't know what it was. I'd visit Blake and see he was OK and I'd chat to Francesca and, on the outside, I'd seem fine. But, on the inside, something wasn't right – something awful had crawled inside me and now it was devouring my very soul.

Every time I got home from a visit, an overwhelming depression would come over me and wouldn't go away. I'd never felt quite like this before, even in the darkest of times. I'd always been able to see some hope, some little light at the end of the rainbow. But now there seemed to be nothing – no belief, no dream, no patch of blue sky in the distance, no straw to clutch at. I don't know why I felt like that, Blake was closer now to being released than ever. But depression is like a black curtain of despair, a sea of sadness, a constant catharsis of hopelessness, worthlessness. Maybe it was a reaction, a kind of post-prison dysthymia, I don't know. It grew stronger with each day and with each lonely night and it frightened me. I wandered round the house in a kind of stupor, as if I was nothing more than a ghost. The need for Blake grew strong and stronger. I just had to be near him. It grew into an obsession, a paranoia – it was an insanity. I would ring the Phoenix Futures at all hours of the night. They always knew it was me.

'Hello, Mrs Civil.'

'Can I please have Blake!'

'You know you can't.'

'Please .. just for one minute!'

'Let us help you.'

'No, I want Blake! I want Blake!'

'Blake's had good therapy today, think of him.'

Then I'd be sorry. Sorry! Sorry! Sorry! Sorry! They'd ask me again if I was alright and I'd say I was, even though I wasn't.

'Tell him I love him.'

'Of course we will. Goodnight.'

I wouldn't hang the phone up immediately. I'd listen to the dead tone for ages, for what seemed like hours, in my melancholic trance. Some nights I didn't sleep at all, just wandered round the house, talking to myself. Then, a night or two later, I'd call the Phoenix rehab again – and have the same conversation over again.

'When can I speak to him?'

'Just a few more days.'

'Is he OK?'

'He's settled and happy.'

'Is he? Is he?'

'You know he is, Mrs Civil.'

Sorry! Sorry! Sorry! Sorry! I wondered what they must think of me – listening to my pathetic diatribe on the other end of their telephone line. That I was crazy? That I was the reason my son was with them? That I was the very worst kind of mother?

Then, one night, they did let me speak to him. I couldn't believe it. It was just amazing. He sounded so different – so strong.

'Listen to me, mum, I know you're having a hard time, but I'll be home soon. Then we'll be together forever .. you, me and the boys.'

I was crying so much I couldn't speak.

'Mum, stop it. Francesca will ring you in a minute. OK?'

'Alright. Sorry. Sorry.'

He told me I'd be able to visit him in a couple of weeks. He said it wouldn't be long now. He said he was doing well and he'd soon be home. He said he'd look after me and never leave me. He told me he loved me, the boys loved me. He told me to stop crying, to try to get a hold of myself.

'I don't know what's wrong with me.'

'Focus, mum. Think of the good times, plan us a holiday .. anywhere you want to go.'

I knew where I wanted to go – to the stars. I wanted to fly to the silver stars with my boys. I began to plan it, for when Blake came home. What had he said to me – "we'll be together forever, you, me and the boys" – and we would be. I'd get it all organised, the means, the method, the time, the place. I saw nothing wrong with what I was thinking. It was a final solution to all my troubles Lord – soon be over!

I have no accurate memory of what I said on the telephone, during those first weeks when Blake was in Sheffield. For years, I'd been blaming this and that and the other for the misery I experienced. I blamed the media, I blamed the person who first introduced Blake to drugs, I blamed Blake himself, I blamed my husbands, I blamed Mitch Winehouse, I blamed Amy. But all the blaming hadn't taken the pain away, hadn't taken the guilt away – and the need to blame myself. I rambled on at myself about it, feeling nothing but fear and misery and loneliness. I wondered if this was how you became a drug-addict, if it was as easy to become dependent upon drugs and it was to become an obsessed psychotic. Or if people were driven to drugs to shut out the terrible waking nightmares that stalked them. Was I any better than the worst "junkie"? Here I was, planning to murder my three sons and myself, because it was the only way I could sleep at night. Because it was the only thing that made any sense to me anymore. Because it was the only way I could get rid of the demon inside myself. Was it like that for Blake? For Amy? Was their pain as bad as the pain I was feeling? If it was, then I couldn't blame them anymore. I know there are many people in this world who have had to deal with a lot more than I have. All I can do is admit that I am weaker than them – and say sorry. Sorry.

I was tired of wandering round the house like a spectre, trying to understand what was wrong with me. Some people choose drugs to overcome the pain, some people choose alcohol, some people choose to make themselves vomit back up everything they've eaten. I chose suicide!

Then something changed.

I was given two phone calls a week. One from me to Blake and one from Blake to me. When we talked, it was as if he knew what was in my mind, I don't know how. I can't explain it. He never actually mentioned the word "suicide", but somehow he knew. Each time I spoke to him on the phone, it was like a therapy session – as if he was my psychiatrist. He was receiving therapy himself and he was passing something of it on to me, not the same kind of therapy, but a gradual will to live. A reason to live.

'Be strong, mum. We need you.'

'But I need you, Blake. I need you!'

'Make sure you go to bed tonight, mum. Promise me.'

'I'll try.'

'Are you smiling?'

'No.'

'Please smile.'

I thought a smile would crack my face in two, it was so difficult to even comprehend. But he'd keep saying it, every time we spoke. "Please smile". Please smile". "Please smile". Eventually, I did.

'Are you smiling?'

'Yes.'

'Good, go to bed with that smile.'

Then, he got Francesca to ring me on the nights I wasn't allowed to speak to him. He told her what to say, how to handle me. And she did, every night. I was in a mess, the black cloud was hanging over me, swirling round me. I couldn't see through it. I could touch the darkness. All I thought about was flying high above that cloud with my boys, flying among the silver stars. It was the only light I could see, that silver light. It became part of my thoughts, every moment of the day. I couldn't wait for Blake to come home so we could fly. Happy and free.

Then he told me to smile. And I did.

The phone calls continued every night, either from Blake or Francesca. He would say Francesca had told him I was wandering round the house, not eating, not sleeping.

'I don't feel good, Blake.'

'What about a pill and a poop?'

It made me smile.

'You must eat, mum. You must eat and sleep .. for me.'

So I began to eat and sleep – as well as smile.

Francesca would speak to me way into the night. We'd talk and cry together. I could feel the strength coming from her, and Blake. And gradually, very gradually, I felt my own strength returning. Blake was always positive, never negative.

'Look for a house for us, mum.'

'Smile, mum.'

'I'll be home soon, mum.'

'Smile, mum.'

'I love you, mum.'

'Smile, mum.'

'You must eat and sleep, mum.'

Smile. I was smiling every time I heard his voice. He told me not to cry anymore. He promised me he hadn't taken any drugs and he never would again. He told me he felt alive again – and I began to feel alive again too. Those are the words that kept me going, that lifted the darkness from my soul, that gave me hope and a reason to live. And Francesca was a true angel. She was only nineteen, but she helped me through my darkest moments and I loved and respected her dearly. She will always be in my heart.

Then one night, during a phone call to Blake, as we were talking about how well he was and how positive and strong he sounded – it came out of the blue.

'You're not still going to kill us all, are you mum?'

I didn't answer for a while – I don't know how long. The breath was completely knocked out of me. How did he know? I'd never said anything. It was as if he'd been reading my mind. I regained my voice. It sounded unsteady.

'No, darling .. I'm not.'

Then he carried on from where we'd left off, without any further reference to suicide, about how wonderful life was and the future that lay ahead of us all. He knew all along, and he gave me back a reason to live every time he rang me – a reason to trust, to believe, to plan, to smile. I saw my image in the mirror and, yes, I was smiling.

I knew it was over.

CHAPTER 18
AN ANGEL ON MY SHOULDER

I wondered many times how I might set the record straight, how I could make it up to Blake for failing him in the first place and thank him for saving me from my suicide obsession. I so wanted to do something, all those times when my heart had gone out to him, when he'd had to read in the press that Amy was with a new boyfriend and had to see pictures of her on this man's arm or that man's arm. She was reported to be off the drugs when she came back from St. Lucia, but the pictures of her looking wasted kept appearing in the papers and her mother and father kept blaming Blake, because they said she was telephoning him. So-called "pals" sold their stories about how she was doing this and doing that, not caring what sort of effect those stories would have on Blake. But I was his mother and Amy was my daughter-in-law – and I did care! I wished that I could do something about those stories and images. I wished I had a voice that everyone would listen to, then I'd tell the truth – the real truth.

Amy was in court on assault charge that allegedly happened the previous September at a charity ball. Some dancer said Amy punched her in the face and shouted –

'Life can't go on. I can't do this anymore!'

Amy had been arrested and investigated after other incidents, but the police had always dropped the charges. This was the first time something had found its way into court. She was smashing drinks at functions and behaving hyper and erratic and Blake was still being blamed for everything she did – even though he wasn't with her when most of it happened.

Sometimes I thought that there was a lesson for me to learn from my son. Maybe I should have been more stoical and not so easily hurt and just let everything go, let it all wash over me. But I'm not as strong as

Blake, I'm not as forgiving nor as philosophical about things and I felt there was another side of the story to be told, a side the newspapers never reported, because it didn't fit with the image they had created for my son. But how could I get my version of events across? Who'd listen to me?

Even though the terrible guilt I'd felt for so long was beginning to retreat, to ebb away slowly, a damaged psyche doesn't mend that easily and I still had my nightmares. I'd loved Giles so much, he was my soul-mate, but my love for Blake was stronger and took over my life and the price I paid for that was to be left on my own. It would have been easy to say this was responsible or that was responsible, just like I'd done so many times before, but I couldn't blame drugs or denial or the tabloids or Mitch Winehouse for my loneliness and self-inflicted solitude, that was my own doing.

I felt like a failure. I'd taken Lance away from Blake, because I thought I was a better parent than him. I'd chosen Giles because I loved him and trusted him to love Blake and that hadn't worked out either. I'd made mistake after mistake and now the chickens had all come home to roost. The choices I'd made had grave consequences for my children and I wanted to make a statement about it, to warn other parents not to do what I had done. Not to make choices that had the effect of driving their children down the wrong path. I wanted to plead with parents to take responsibility for the lives of their children, before things got out of hand. I was responsible for Blake choosing drugs, but I still didn't fully understand what had driven him to destroy his youth. I still didn't know what he was running from, what pain he was hiding. Maybe he'd tried to tell me, but I didn't hear. We were supposed to get it all out in the open at Life Works, but that never happened. I'd said "sorry" a thousand times, to Blake, when he wasn't there to hear me – when it was too late. I wanted to tell other parents not to be conceited like I used to be, to have the courage to admit and the patience to listen. If there was only some way I could tell people what I felt.

But there wasn't, so all I could do was wallow in my contrition and continue to silently blame myself.

Giles blamed Blake.

He blamed him for my depression and my obsession and my isolation and my neglect of him. But he forgot I was that thing which defies definition – a mother, so there could never be any other outcome. I thought about Giles a lot at this time and I wished he was still with us, with me and the boys. I asked myself if the price was worth the persistence, if my determination was worth the dénouement. Giles would always express his reservations to me.

'I hope Blake never lets you down, Georgette. You've lost everything, for him. I just hope he appreciates the sacrifice you've made.'

And it wasn't just my sacrifice – the boys had lost their father, that hurt me more than anything else. I told myself that time is a healer, a dimmer of memory, a distorter of light – but it didn't help. I wondered what would have been the outcome if I'd made different decisions, and my conclusions were always the same – it was a fait accompli from the start, it was kismet. I couldn't have done anything else. I'd have stood by Blake, no matter what the cost and no matter what the circumstances, because a child can have many moons in his life, but only one mother.

In March 2009, Amy said in a magazine that she still loved Blake and wanted him to move into her new house in North London with her. She said that was part of her plan all along. I wondered what plan that was? Despite not contesting the divorce proceedings, she said she wouldn't let him do it, because he was her male alter ego and they were perfect for each other. Maybe they did have a plan, between them. I wasn't convinced even then that he'd go through with the divorce. He was having second thoughts and I was sure he'd call it off before the decree nisi. I had mixed feelings about that, Blake was so much better and it was reported that Amy was recovering as well, after her stay in St. Lucia. So, maybe divorce was the best thing for both of them.

Sadly, Francesca's mother found out that she was still visiting Blake with me, and they were forced apart – they remained good friends, but the closeness they had then wasn't allowed to flourish. I could understand that Francesca's family had plans for their daughter and those plans didn't include a recovering drug-addict. But people would always judge and, for me, that was the hardest part. I knew that, whatever Blake did in life from then on, he would always be "the addict", he would never be just "Blake". I realised his journey would never end, quite apart from his fight against addiction, he would always be proving himself to people who didn't understand who he really was. I wanted so much to be able to tell everybody who he really was – what I saw in him and what Amy saw in him. I wanted the world to know the real Blake Fielder-Civil.

My mother had suggested to me several times that I should write a book, to share the sadness I had felt, and was still feeling, during this time with other parents of drug-addicted children.

'You might be able to help them, Georgette.'

'Who'd be interested, mum?'

'Parents .. mothers, like you.'

But I knew I would never be able to write a book, I was a hairdresser, not an author. So I put the idea out of my head, until one day in early June 2009, when my friend Pam called.

'There's this clairvoyant, Georgette, she's really good. D'you fancy it?'

Pam was into that sort of thing, psychics and fortune-tellers and séances and stuff. I wasn't, but I thought I'd tag along – I might even get a laugh out of it and I could certainly do with cheering up.

'OK, what do I do?'

'Nothing, you just send her a text message to say you're coming with me, that's all.'

So I did. And, a few days later, I was on my way to see the woman with Pam. When I said it wasn't my thing, I mean I had an open mind. People who go to psychics are looking for answers, for reasons why things are the way they are and, if they're lucky, to find out how things might pan out in the future. I believed that, if you didn't know these things yourself, nobody else could tell you. But .. I suppose there are more things in heaven and earth, Horatio. I was cautious, but I had nothing to lose.

Pam went in first, while I waited outside in a reception room. I thought I could hear her sobbing and I wondered what she'd been told to make her do that. Suddenly, I didn't like it. I wanted to run – if it made Pam sad, what would it do to me? But, despite my trepidation, part of me wanted to stay. Maybe it was just morbid curiosity, or maybe something was holding me there, I don't know. Then it was my turn and I went inside. It was a room like any other room, only filled with thank-you cards from clients – and candles, many aromatic candles. They smelled of calmness and reassurance, so I relaxed a little. I'd expected a Gypsy, with large earrings and a crystal ball, but it wasn't anything like that. It was so very peaceful and unintimidating and the clairvoyant herself looked like any other fortysomething woman. She asked me not to speak, not to say anything or ask any questions until she was finished. That way, I couldn't give her any clues as to who I was or why I was there. So I said nothing, just sat there stony-faced, listening. But my nonchalant expression didn't last for long because, after just a few preliminary minutes, she said the word "book". I started to pay attention.

'They're showing me a book. They've shown it to me twice now. I'll try to find out more.'

She seemed as if she was listening to someone I couldn't hear, some invisible voice that was in the room with us. I tried to look inscrutable, unperturbed, so I wouldn't give my curiosity away.

'There's a presence here, someone who passed a long time ago. He's family and he says he's sorry for all your pain. But, he says, there's an angel on your shoulder.'

I immediately looked at both my shoulders, but could see nothing.

'The angel will help you find your sanctuary.'

I couldn't believe what I was hearing.

Many years previous, before it became so complicated, I used to consider my life – what it meant, what I'd like to do more than anything else, if I had the choice. Long before the homeless man in the doorway, I'd wanted to do something for people like that, not just give them ten pounds as I was passing, but something more substantial – more permanent. I hadn't mentioned this to anyone, except Blake, when he was young. I told him if I ever got the chance, I would open a place – a house, I don't know, maybe a rehab or a refuge or something. Somewhere for them to go, a safe house, where they would have a chance to pick themselves up and look at their lives and then, if they wanted, to rejoin society. This clairvoyant could not possibly have known about that.

'You've been wanting to do something .. a dream. You have a dream, but it won't always be a dream.'

I didn't say a word, just sat there, waiting for more.

'They're showing me this book again .. now there's writing in it. I believe it's a book you're going to write. The money you make from this book will help make your dream happen.'

She couldn't possibly have known about the book either. Only me and my mother knew about that.

'A man will be involved with this book. You'll know who he is, the minute you hear his voice. It will be a distinctive voice.'

I hadn't a clue who that could be. But she carried on, without me opening my mouth to confirm or deny anything. She talked about my heartache, about my boys and about Giles. Everything she said was completely accurate.

'Your book is connected .. it's part of everything. It will change minds. It will be read in many languages.'

She said the presence from my past told her the angel on my shoulder was my guardian, it would protect and guide me. I found this difficult to believe, as nobody or nothing had been protecting me up to now. She also said my tutelary angel's was name was Gazardiel and it was an angel of new beginnings.

When the clairvoyant finished, she didn't ask me to say whether she was right or wrong, which was just as well, because I was at a loss for words. I didn't even ask her name, I just thanked her and left with Pam. I was amazed, she was just so accurate about all the details of my life, I couldn't believe it. It was as if she'd been my best friend all my life and I'd confided completely in her and, if she was right about everything else, maybe she was right about the book too – and the angel on my shoulder? I thought about the presence from my past that she'd mentioned and I believed that, if someone was there, it could only be my grandfather. He was the only dead person I was ever that close to. I spoke to Blake about the experience.

'I saw a clairvoyant the other day.'

'Oh mum! Why?'

'Don't know. Pam made me.'

'No she didn't! Nobody makes you do anything.'

I'd been thinking about the book, ever since the psychic mentioned it – and the mysterious man who would be involved with it.

'She said I was going to write a book .. and that I had a dream. The book will help make the dream come true. I know what she meant, Blake.'

'So do I, mum. She meant you house of lost souls.'

'You remember?'

'I remember. When I was young, we would see people in doorways and you'd say, if you had more money, you'd buy a big house and those people would come to you and you'd help them get themselves together.'

That was my dream. I kept thinking about the book, but I didn't know how to write it. I didn't know where to start. I needed someone to help me – a ghost writer or something, isn't that what they called themselves? I got onto the internet and contacted a few, yet every time they spoke to me, their voice didn't sound right. I don't know why, but it just felt wrong. After several weeks of searching, I was ready to give up. If it was grandfather who was trying to help me, then he had a funny way of showing it – and, if there was an angel on my shoulder, it wasn't doing much tutelage. One night I sat at my table. It was late and I was tired, so I closed down the computer. I spoke to the empty room.

'Grandfather, if you're there, help me. Gazardiel, if you're there .. help me. I'm tired searching. You told me to write a book, but I need some help.'

The empty room didn't answer, so I decided to make a drink, smoke a cigarette and go to bed. While I was doing this, something in my head told me to start up the computer again and have one final go at it. I wasn't optimistic, but it felt as if something or someone was telling me to do it. So I did. I switched the computer back on, sat in front of it and spoke to the empty room again.

'Well, guardian angel, here we go. Do your bit.'

I googled something really silly – "writer wanted", or something vague like that – the first thing that came into my head. I didn't expect it to work. I waited for a response. Then a name came up on the screen.

"John F McDonald" and a web address. I went onto the site and looked at the photo of this man. Something drew me to it. I looked at it for a long time. Was he the one the clairvoyant had told me about? There was a phone number on the website. I wanted to ring it, but I was scared. It was late, what would I say? The more I looked at the picture, the more I felt I knew him.

'OK, grandfather .. here we go.'

I could hear the phone ringing at the other end. Once, twice, three times. I almost hung up.

'Hello.'

'John F McDonald?'

'That's me.'

'The writer?'

'So I've been called.'

The voice was distinctive, unusual. It sounded American, but it wasn't – it was more than that. It was a mixture of several accents. Unusual. Soft, with a kind of lilt to it. This was him, I knew it immediately. This was the man the psychic had spoken about. I didn't know what to say.

'Hi, I'm Georgette.'

'How are you, Georgette? What can I do for you?'

'I want to write a book.'

I had a stupid smile on my face, as if I was a teenager again, talking to some boy on the phone about a first date. But, within a few minutes, we were chatting like we'd known each other all our lives. We arranged to meet in London on Monday 27th July 2009.

I felt a bit foolish, as I boarded the train for Kings Cross. Who would be interested in my book? Who did I think I was? I wanted to get off and run back home. But I remembered the clairvoyant and how I'd come to get in touch with JohnF, so I decided to go through with it. You can doubt yourself like that, in the cold light of day, can't you? You can doubt everything. Was the psychic a fraud? Did she find out about my book and my dream in some clever way that wasn't apparent to me? Did she trick me? But what about the computer? I was ready to give up my search, until I spoke to my grandfather – if it was my grandfather – and then it happened. I had to go through with it, now that I'd come this far. What did I have to lose?

There was nobody waiting for me when I got to Kings Cross. My heart sank. Where was he? Why wasn't he there? I didn't know what to do for a few minutes. The station was full of strangers, all coming or going – all moving through, or waiting for trains. I looked round, but I couldn't see anyone who resembled the picture on the website. Then, something told me to go across to the information centre and ask them announce that Georgette Civil was waiting by platform five for John McDonald. I heard the announcement as I made my way back to the platform. Within a very short time, he was there, standing beside me. He seemed to appear out of nowhere. The minute I saw him, I knew somehow that this was the man the clairvoyant had told me about.

'Do you believe in angels?'

I don't know why I asked that question. It just came out. I felt so stupid.

'"Angels are bright still, though the brightest fell" .. that's from Macbeth, Georgette. They're there if you believe they are.'

This was the man who would help me to write my book.

We went to a bar in Euston Road and spent half the day talking. He didn't take any notes or tape anything I was saying and I thought, maybe he doesn't want to do it. What will I do if he says no? But that was the way we were going to work together – easily, informally, like close friends. He said this first meeting was just to establish whether we could get on with each other – it was very important to like each other, as we would be working together for a long time. The other thing was trust. He said it was important that we trusted each other, after all, I would be baring my soul to him and he would be trusting me to go through with the project, right to the end – no matter how difficult it got.

By the time I had to return to Kings Cross to catch my train, we knew enough about each other to agree that I should write this book. JohnF advised me to start it at a turning point – the day I received that fateful phone call from Amy. He said the book would take on a life of its own from there on. And it did. It became very important to me – not just for the realisation of my dream, but also to share my pain, and joy, with others who might be in the same situation as I was. I wanted to tell people that, no matter how dark and desolate life seems, there should always be hope. Suicide is not an answer, you must face your demons and overcome them. It's difficult, God knows I understand that, and it's easy for people to pontificate when it's not happening to them. But there is light, if you just look for it – and most of the time it will come from your child, no matter how unlikely that may seem. Just look at them and smile.

Because, when you smile, you're beautiful!

In the meantime, Blake had gone ahead with the divorce, despite what he felt deep down inside. The decree nisi was granted on 16th July 2009, while he was still in rehab at Phoenix Futures in Sheffield. Neither Blake nor Amy attended the hearing, nor did I or any of Amy's family. But I remembered that Amy had mentioned a "plan" and that put the seed of doubt in my mind. I wondered if I'd been right, that time I told Blake I could write his script for him and he'd smiled back at me.

'Clever mum.'

After I started writing the book, I felt a strong presence in the house. Was grandfather with me, or was it all in my head? Sometimes it seemed like I was going crazy. I'd been crazy before, so why not again now? Other people started coming to me, my great-uncle Tommy, who was killed during the First World War and other vague presences who were obscure and even a little frightening. Tommy spoke about my sadness, my future, joy to come, my house of lost souls and my book.

I was happy, for the first time in a long while.

Then, on 27th August, I was served with a writ from Mitch Winehouse, for giving one of Amy's letters to a tabloid newspaper. The writ was officially from Amy, but I guessed it was really from Mitch – in other words, the writ had "Mitch" written all over it. I wondered what was going on. Shortly before, a piece had appeared in the News Of The World about my book and I wondered if this was a warning. The letter had been quoted in the tabloid a long time earlier, so what was the big deal about it now? There was also a comment from Amy's "spokeswoman" in the News Of The World that she was very disappointed that Blake's family were airing aspects of her private life in public. Amy never made that comment and her "spokeswoman" had to be Mitch. I was convinced this was a warning from Mitch, not to write anything about him in my book. The person who served the writ said he thought the whole thing was ridiculous and he wished me good luck with my project.

On 28th August 2009, the day after I was served with the writ, the divorce became final with a decree absolute. None of us were in court to witness the event.

Blake's road to self-determination had begun.

But that wasn't all, strange things began to happen. Like, some anonymous person sent me e-mails from Blake to Amy and from Amy to Blake. I couldn't identify the sender and God only knows how they acquired them or why they sent them to me. The messages were vows of love, which seemed strange, just after a divorce. I put it down to somebody getting into either Blake's or Amy's e-mail account and trying to cause mischief. As well as that, all the passwords to my bank account were suddenly removed. The bank couldn't explain how this happened and I never found out why, but what looked like the word "valere" appeared on a temporary statement I printed out from the automatic machine at my local branch. It was put down to being a smudge of ink and not an actual word by the bank, so I let it go. These were just small insignificant things on their own but, all together, they formed an eerie counterpoint to the feelgood emanations of the clairvoyant and, for a while, I wondered if I shouldn't have dabbled with forces I knew nothing about.

Spooky!

But, despite these strange anomalies, I was determined to carry on writing. Blake said he hoped the book would bring me peace. The spirit-people told me I'd be moving house, to someplace where I'd be loved instead of hated.

And, I thought, who knows?

The future is such a fickle thing!

CHAPTER 19
A KIND OF FREEDOM

Blake was released on licence from Phoenix Futures on 14th September 2009. It was Amy's birthday, she was twenty-six. He'd served more time than any of the other men involved in the conspiracy, but at last he was free. When I say "free", I mean it was his first night where he wasn't under a detention regime of one kind or another. A condition of Blake's release on licence was that he could not come home to live with me – I was never given an adequate reason for this and I wondered if it was the authorities way of punishing me further for being a bad mother. Anyway, we found a nice apartment in Sheffield, with a balcony, and Blake got himself a job in a local gym. The future seemed bright, for a change. But it wasn't long before the tabloids and Mitch Winehouse were at it again, as I knew they inevitably would. Photos of Amy appeared in the papers with white powder on her face and Mitch attributed the blame for this to Blake's influence, even though he hadn't seen Amy since his release and regardless of the fact that irresponsible statements like that could jeopardise his embryonic and fragile freedom.

Blake and Amy did begin to telephone each other – every day, and I knew my prediction of a spring wedding would probably come true. I was so happy, because Blake was so happy – or seemed so happy. The newspapers kept on reporting things like Amy's "shambolic" gigs, where she, according to them, had to be dragged offstage shouting "I love you, Blake!" She also admitted that the reports of her with other men while Blake was in prison were all just part of a "front", to keep the truth of her love for Blake a secret from her family. I was inclined to believe that because, when Blake asked her to put a stop to the law-suit her father had initiated against me in her name, she did it – immediately!

Then, in mid September, it was reported that Mitch had "caught" Blake in bed with Amy. The papers said Mitch was sick with worry, after finding his daughter in bed with her "no-good" ex-husband. Anyone reading this rubbish could be excused for thinking that Amy was sixteen, instead of twenty-six and that Blake was some kind of demon from hell, out to steal her virginity. The papers went on to say that Mitch "threw Blake out" and threatened to "punch his lights out". Blake was reported to have "begged Mitch not to hit him" as he was being "chucked out". The ubiquitous "source" said – "the man responsible for dragging her into the gutter is crawling back into her life". The truth of the episode was that Amy had asked Blake to come see her. They had a fabulous night together – until Mitch showed up next morning, making threats.

'It was awful, mum. I was with my wife .. the next thing her father turned up, calling me all those names. Poor Amy was screaming at him to stop.'

Mitch then goaded Blake to hit him, knowing full well it would be straight back to prison for Blake if he did.

'He kept saying .. "go on Blake, hit me!" I just told him to grow up.'

Mitch had taken the precaution of bringing two big bodyguards with him, just in case he might have to actually back up his words. Blake didn't hit him, he kept his cool and I was proud of the way he reacted under such provocation. Blake left with his head held high, having behaved like the mature adult he is. He was not "chucked out", and all Mitch Winehouse succeeded in doing was to alienate his daughter further and contribute to the catalogue of stress he constantly placed her under.

This proved to me that Blake had grown up over the past two years. He was full of confidence and a new kind of self-respect and self-belief.

'Maybe what happened was for the best, mum. Who knows where I would be now? How did I ever get myself into that mess?'

I felt better than I had in years. It seemed that I could look forward to tomorrow with a smile, my son looked so fit and handsome and I told myself how lucky I was. He and Amy were going on Facebook and declaring their love for each other, Amy also telephoned and spoke to Harry and Fred.

'Amy loves the boys, mum, she always has.'

'I know that, darling. The boys love her too.'

'She loves you too, mum. You know that.'

'Yes, I do. I love her as well.'

She told the boys she cried when her father dropped the ridiculous law suit against me. She told them how much she missed them and they were so glad to hear from her again. They really loved her and Blake so much – he was like a surrogate father to them, rather than a big brother. They listened to him and respected him and, even though he'd made mistakes in his own life, he was able to pass on some of the lessons he'd learned to the younger boys. That was the thing with us, we were never afraid to say "I love you". It was a natural thing to us, to show our feelings – even if they were sometimes tinged with sadness or anger. We never had to justify ourselves to each other, we just said it as it was.

Amy sent me a note –

"Hi momsie, I was so pleased when Mitchell
said he wasn't suing you. I cried. Let's meet
in secret, how fab would that be? Love you
all so much. Our boy looks so handsome.
Kisses, Amy"

I called her after that. We hadn't spoke in a long time and I was a bit nervous ringing her. But it felt right. She picked the phone up.

'Amy, is that you?'

'Yes.'

'Amy, it's Blake's mum.'

'Georgette? Georgette! Georgette!'

It was so good to hear her voice again. She seemed glad to hear me too.

'I love Blake, nobody could love him more than me.'

'I know that, honey.'

'Momsie .. you know we're going to get back together?'

'Yes, I know that, Amy.'

'We can't be together yet, but we soon will. He's the most amazing person in the world. I love him so much.'

'He loves you too, Amy. I only wish your dad and I could be friends.'

'Don't hold your breath, momsie .. I told him about you and Giles.'

'What did he say?'

'He said he was really sorry. I think he meant it.'

'I'm sure he did, Amy.'

We chatted on for ages about how much we'd missed each other and how much we loved each other, and we really meant it. Amy always had this ability to make me feel kind of warm inside – it was a silly feeling, really – but, it was like you could feel her sincerity, even on the end of a telephone line. I knew the bad old times, when we were distant from each other, were over at last.

'Blake will be OK, momsie. I'm always there for him, don't worry.'

'Thank you, Amy.'

'You're a strong person, momsie .. and sensitive, just like Blake.'

I made a wish that she'd be happy. I so wanted for her to be happy.

We'd all been to hell and back, and now we were smiling again. But it wasn't easy bringing up two teenage boys on my own, without a father. The boys were confused and worried about everything that had happened, and about everything that might happen in the future. They didn't want things to return to the way they were before. But Blake was back now and he reassured me when things got a bit tough.

'Mum, if you have trouble with the boys tell me. OK?'

'Will do.'

'I'm here for you.'

'I know you are.'

'Never hurt them, even if you're stressed. Let me know first, then I can have a word with them. Don't say things you'll regret, just because you think you can't cope.'

'I promise, darling.'

I didn't feel angry or bitter towards Giles any more. The darkness seemed to be gone and it was a time to forgive and forget – a time for reconciliation. The signs from my spirits were good and I felt at peace.

Then I had a call from Blake – he sounded upset.

'Mum, I've had probation round today. They came with photos of the assault on King.'

'Why did they do that?'

'So I can never forget what I did. I've done more time than any of the others involved, why won't they leave me alone?'

'I'll come over.'

'It's because I'm married to Amy, mum, that's what it's all about. Mike Brown is free, Kelly is free, Kennedy only got community service. I got the lot! What more do they want from me?'

He was right, and we both knew it – he'd paid the highest price of all for getting into a fight on a Saturday night and, even though he was supposed to be free, he was still paying that price – and so was I. If he hadn't been married to Amy, he wouldn't have been set up the way he was and probably would never have gone to prison. I found it all so depressing – while the probation people were busy harassing him, a child up the road could be suffering because of their misguided sense of priority. Blake was at a critical time in his recovery, their irresponsible actions could have been the catalyst that made him relapse – and they should have known that.

Maybe they did.

'Mum, Amy's in hospital .. and they're even trying to stop me seeing her.'

'They can't!'

'They can!'

I so much wanted to go to him, but he told me not to come, he'd deal with it himself. I didn't sleep that night, I lay awake worrying, in case he relapsed. I wanted so badly for February 2010 to come, so we could all be really free of this nightmare that had controlled our every waking moment for the past two years!

It turned out that Amy was in hospital having breast enhancements that were rumoured to have cost £35k, so it was nothing too serious – just as well. She later made a guest appearance on Strictly Come Dancing, to promote her god-daughter's singing career, so I knew she was OK. Blake stayed strong, despite the provocation of the probation service and, although I knew I would probably lose my driving licence, things began to calm down again. I went over to Sheffield and spent the day with Blake. We had a wonderful time, it was like the old days together. We remembered the good times and we laughed and tried to forget the bad times. At the back of my mind, however, I couldn't help wondering what tomorrow would bring. What would happen if Blake and Amy remarried, as now seemed very likely? But nothing in life is guaranteed and, whatever the future held, I had Blake today. I decided to let it be and live in the moment – tomorrow would take care of itself.

Blake didn't like me contacting the spirit world, or talking about my guardian angel. He said it was a dangerous obsession, but I had to have some outlet – some means of being in touch with my destiny, even if I couldn't control it. So, I continued to attend séances and ouija-board sessions without telling him. These sessions reassured me that things would turn out for the best and, although I'm sure a lot of people won't agree with me, I believed in them. I called it my "spook club".

Amy telephoned Harry, to wish him a happy birthday. She told him to be a good boy and she'd send him £200 for his birthday. She'd appeared in the papers wearing a pink shirt with the words "Blake's Girl" embroidered on it – further proof that they would be back together soon. When I looked at Blake, he seemed happy, healthy and full of life. Yet I had to ask myself at times, "is he really at peace?" Then, it was just me being me, wasn't it? I couldn't believe things could go right for us for a change – it had been so long since they did. He told me he was scared sometimes to be alone at night, and that bothered me. There were still a few pieces of the jigsaw to go, before we could be truly free. Moving house was one of them, and I resolved to be out of Claypole by Christmas. The other thing was – sometimes I would wake up screaming in the middle of the night after having a bad dream. It seemed like a bad dream but, after I woke, I could still feel some sort of presence in the room. It frightened the boys and they told Blake about it. He blamed the "spook club" and said that, as a Christian, I shouldn't be involved in things like that. I told him I'd stop, but I knew I wouldn't.

'Mum, this spirit thing is bad for you, just like drugs are bad for me.'

'It's not the same thing.'

'It is! It would be so easy for me to give in and do a line, but I know one would lead to another and another and I wouldn't know when to stop. You don't know when to stop with this spirit thing, and it's becoming an addiction.'

'No it's not, Blake. It's harmless.'

The News of the World ran a story about Blake being involved with a nightclub stripper in Sheffield. I knew this would upset Amy and it gave me an excuse to go see Blake. He seemed uneasy when I got there. I worried when he was a bit down – I prayed he would be strong enough to cope.

'It's just a story, mum. You know the papers will print anything any idiot tells them. They didn't even have the right photograph.'

'It will upset Amy.'

'Amy's not upset. She knows the truth.'

I knew he was right. But I had to get round to the subject of Giles somehow and this was all I had. He seemed to know, somehow, what was coming.

'Anyway, mum, you're the one who made me divorce Amy. You said it was for the best.'

'I didn't make you do it, Blake. And it was for the best.'

'How would you know what's for the best?'

That was it! There was only one way to do this.

'Tell me about Giles.'

Blake looked at me for a moment, shaking his head. I thought he was going to get up and walk away, but he didn't. He just sighed – a long, long sigh.

'He hated me, mum.'

The words just came out of his mouth in a kind of whisper, as if they'd been there on the tip of his tongue for years – as if he'd been holding them back all that time, but now he couldn't do it any longer.

'He beat me when you weren't there. I did try to tell you, but you didn't believe me.'

I didn't remember him trying to tell me. I would have believed him if he'd told me. How could he say something like that? More was to come.

'He threw me down the stairs, mum. He kicked me and squashed my head. He shouted at me all the time, like I was an animal. He made me feel worthless. He made me hate myself. That's why I left home, to get away from him.'

I was stunned. What could I say. I tried to remember, tried to think back – it was so long ago, so much had happened. I couldn't imagine Giles hurting Blake, he was so good with him – when we were together.

I had a vague memory of something – of Blake saying something to me many years ago.

I think it was when we were living at Rippingale, Bourne. Was that when Giles changed? At first – in the beginning – he and Blake loved each other deeply. He was the father Blake never had. Then Harry came – was that when things began to change? I tried to remember – something – anything.

'Giles was horrible to me when you were at work, mum. He chased me round the house.'

'I remember talking to him about you at that time, darling.'

'He used to say I was a drama queen.'

'I'm so sorry, Blake.'

'You didn't listen to me!'

'Giles said .. he said drugs make you paranoid .. they make you imagine things ..'

'Drugs again, mum, always the drugs .. an excuse for everything! Maybe it's the other way round. Maybe everything is an excuse for the drugs?'

Suddenly, his face lost its edginess. He smiled and put his arms round me.

'It's not so good for me to dwell on all this stuff, mum. I'm just happy to still have you and Harry and Fred. Let's just leave it at that.'

I went back to Claypole in a daze. I couldn't sleep. Blake's words kept repeating themselves over and over in my head. I'd made a mistake when I married Lance and the courts had to sort that one out for me. Then I chose Giles to help me bring up Blake. Surely I didn't get it wrong again? He was a kind man, a good man – a man who loved his family. I thought back – Blake was doing well in a good school, the younger boys were in a private nursery, Giles was a teacher, we had a nice home and a good life.

And the darkness came slowly back.

I began to feel strange again – after being so happy. I tried to put it out of my head. I should still be happy, with Blake free of drugs and free from prison. If the stuff about Giles was true, then it wasn't happening anymore, because he was gone. I was moving out of Claypole at last and my book was coming along well. What was there not to be happy about? But the old sadness was growing inside me again, and I didn't seem to be able to do anything about it. This stuff about Giles had woken the demon that had lay dormant inside me since Blake first went to rehab.

Everything seemed to have an edginess about it. Cracks were beginning to appear in my little cocoon of happiness again – hairline fractures that allowed the old depression in. It wasn't so much that Blake was getting back with Amy – that didn't worry me too much, I knew it was destiny and nothing could stop it. But other things, that I normally might not have noticed, began to loom large and have that distinct mephitis of doom about them – he had an ear infection – he felt insecure – he didn't know what was wrong with him. Small things that meant nothing individually, but which added up to a sense of impending disaster that sent me back into my melancholia.

'Mum, I don't know what's the matter. My ears are hurting .. I feel fed up .. it's stupid, but I wish I was back in prison.'

'Never say that, Blake. I'll come over to you.'

'No mum, I'm just being silly.'

'Tell me what the matter is.'

'It's nothing.'

I was really worried, in case it all got the better of him and he went for the security blanket of the drugs. But what could I do? We were in different parts of the country. If only the probation people had allowed him to come home, I could have been there for him all the time – when things got tough, when things got rough. As it was, he didn't have me and he didn't have Amy – he had to do it all on his own. The feeling of dread in the pit of my stomach grew. What if it all got too much for him? Would we ever be a normal family again? Would all the shit begin again? Would it matter where I went, would anywhere else be any different to Claypole? I tried to tell myself to stay happy and live in the moment, but the growing feeling of trepidation wouldn't let me. The old depression came back with a vengeance – I could feel the fear, smell it. I knew I couldn't cope with it again, I couldn't be in that hell again. The boys became nervous near me, the paranoia seemed to emanate from me like the tongue of some monstrous chameleon, wrapping itself round them and pulling them towards oblivion.

'What are you going to do, Mum?'

'We have to do what we have to do, darlings.'

I could feel myself drifting back to the image of us all flying in the silver sky – all holding hands and laughing and I began to think about the old alternative again. It was the final option. It was peace of mind. It was security against the future, against the unknown. Was I being a coward, or just simply mad?

I felt so bloody tired.

CHAPTER 20
THE REMAINS OF THE YEAR

I was having so many nightmares again. I asked myself if maybe Blake was right, maybe I was messing with the spirit world too much? But it wasn't that, it was the uncertainty of my life, the not-knowing-what-was-going-to-happen of my life, the worrying about what might be going to happen. Would Blake go back on the drugs? If he remarried Amy, he'd go back into that lifestyle, the celebrity lifestyle – the pressure to take drugs would be enormous, the opportunities would be everywhere. Would the nightmare begin all over again? Would Harry and Fred make the same mistakes as their brother? They were under so much pressure, my younger boys. I began wandering round the house again at night, not eating and not sleeping. It felt as if I was sleepwalking – it even looked as if I was sleepwalking. My eyes would be open and my arms outstretched in front of me. But I was wide awake.

The more I spoke to Amy on the phone, the more I remembered that call, so long ago, when she said those words –

'Blake's been arrested.'

The past was still haunting me. I trusted them, Blake and Amy, and I loved them both. But I also feared for them. Blake was right when he told me I knew nothing about drugs, about the affects they had on a person, the hold they had. But I knew about the heartache they could bring. The thought of it haunted me and I feared for the future. I had faith in Blake and Amy, but I had no faith in the people who could influence them, nor in the media animal that would inevitably stalk them.

All the things I'd done wrong came back to haunt me as well — Giles – the denial – the despair. Would it all happen again? Was I still doing things wrong? I gave Blake no boundaries when he was younger, I believed his happiness was all that mattered. I could see now that this, along with the other mistakes I'd made, contributed to his downfall. I tried to forget the bad things – tried to remember the good things, tried to leave yesterday behind and look forward to tomorrow. I told myself to do it. I told myself I should just let Blake go, let him live his own life now and let him be responsible for the consequences of his actions. Easier said than done! What if he relapsed? What if something happened to make him go back on the drugs? It was such a tenuous thing, his rehabilitation. What if I did something wrong again? Did the addiction have more power than me, could it influence Blake more than I could? Was heroin more powerful than a mother's love – could cocaine defeat the strongest of bonds? I prayed each night that, when the morning came, some brightness would come with it.

The only bit of sunshine was Amy, when she rang me.

'Forget all the crap, momsie, Blake and I will be alright.'

'I hope so, Amy.'

'You'll see. Just wait till he's free of licence.'

That's what I wanted more than anything, for him to be completely free – wasn't it? Then I thought to myself, being on licence is the only barrier between him and the drugs again. Then I wasn't so sure.

'Nobody loves Blake more than me, momsie .. not even you.'

I couldn't believe that. She couldn't – could she?

'I told Mitchell about you and Giles.'

'Did you, Amy?'

'He said he was sorry.'

'I believe you.'

'Be happy, momsie, I just want for you to be happy.'

'I'm writing a book, Amy. You're in it.'

'That's great. Do what makes you happy.'

'And Blake .. and Giles ..'

'Forget about the past. Try to focus on the future.'

I was focusing on the future, that was the problem. I knew Blake and Amy would be together, that was inevitable, but would the drugs be with them as well? Her voice was comforting when she called, in that way of hers – that way which was unique to her – that Amy way. Mitch Winehouse and I did bring up two drug-addicts, but there was another side to them that nobody saw. There was a beautiful side to them that was sensitive and kind and fragile and could be very easily destroyed. Perhaps somewhere amongst all the wrong things, we did something right as well. After all Blake and Amy had been through, they still had the ability to smile and forgive and hope and love. Perhaps Mitch and I could learn from them – what the word "love" really meant?

But the darkness remained and I began to think more and more about us flying in the silver sky – the four of us. It grew large inside me, the longing. I thought about it all the time and I was ready to give in, to succumb to its appeal – to do what Hamlet suggested, to die, to sleep – no more – to end the heartache – the silver sky – the silver stars. Then Amy would ring me and bring me back from the brink – from the edge.

'Blake and I are planning a home together, momsie.'

'What about Mitch, Amy? What about your father?'

'Fuck him!'

'He might ruin it all .. like ..'

'I won't let him, momsie. It won't be like before.'

'Won't it, Amy? Won't it?'

'It won't.'

And I believed her, while she was speaking to me, while she was on the other end of the phone. But, when she hung up, the doubts came back and it seemed it might be just like before – even worse. What if Blake was fitted up again, only this time for something even more serious? What if he was sent back to prison – for five years, or ten years, or even longer? I knew I couldn't go through it all again, and neither could the boys. So, the thoughts of suicide returned when Amy hung up the phone. The doubts came back and the darkness in my heart grew blacker and blacker.

Until one day she called me and made me laugh. It was like when Blake called me from rehab that earlier time and made me smile – when he and Francesca had brought me back to the real world from the limbo in which I was languishing. Now it was Amy who made me laugh and see the sun again.

The conversation started like any other.

'Momsie, the best day of my life was when I married Blake.'

'I know Amy .. you told me.'

'I know I let him down, I could have been a better wife.'

'Perhaps .. but we can't go back, can we?'

I was thinking that I could have been a better mother.

'You were lost at the time, Amy. You were in the grip of addiction, just like Blake. I don't blame you .. or Blake. It's life, isn't it?'

'We've learned a lot, momsie.'

'Blake told me not to forget the past, Amy, because the past makes us what we are today.'

'No, momsie, it's what we've learned from the past that makes us what we are, not the past itself.'

'Are you sure, Amy?'

She must have sensed the sadness in my voice. She paused. There was silence on the phone line for a moment. I thought she'd hung up. Then –

'Do you think my boobs look silly?'

She just came out with it. It was like something a little child would say, totally candid and honest and innocent. I started to laugh. I laughed and laughed and laughed. I could hear Amy laughing with me on the other end of the line. I laughed until tears came from my eyes, then I cried – with happiness.

'No, my darling, I don't. You look wonderful.'

It was as easy as that. This time, when she hung up, the darkness didn't come back. I thought about what she said and I laughed again. Every time her words came into my mind I laughed – her childlike words, her innocent words. It might be hard for you to understand, it was such a simple thing. Her words reminded me that there was so much beauty in the world, despite all the misery – that there was so much honesty in the world, despite all the lies. Such simple, honest, childlike words – but they had the ability to make me laugh. They were so beautiful. She was so beautiful. She was truly my spiritual daughter.

It was different after that. I felt different. I kept the laughter in my heart and it exorcised me. Amy rang me every day and we laughed together every day, sometimes for hours. She was so full of hope and love, so full of understanding and naiveté. We laughed about silly things, girlish things, things that nobody else would laugh at, things that only our shared sense of humour would find funny. And every day I grew stronger, and stronger – until I could talk about life again. Until I could think about the future again, without thinking about the past.

'I wish I could be with Blake, momsie. I want to look after him.'

'He's fine, Amy. He's good.'

'We had the best time ever in America. I hope we can go again.'

'I don't think Blake can go to America, not with his criminal record.'

It was like we'd come full circle, Amy and I, only this time we both had more understanding of who we were – who we really were.

'I hope your dad and I can be friends one day, Amy.'

'That could take a long time, momsie.'

'I know. But, for now, I'm just happy you and I are friends.'

'Me too!'

We always ended our conversations with "love you" – and we did.

I found a new house outside the village of Claypole and near to my business. The worst seemed to be over. Blake and I even began to be able to talk about his childhood and the things that happened, without the memories causing trauma. He confided that he loved Giles deeply, he was the father that Blake never had. But things changed when Harry was born and we moved to Surrey. Blake hated that school and things just went wrong and he said it was only a matter of time before he began to believe it was his fault. But Giles was my soulmate and mentor at that time, and I believed everything would be fine. Then, one day, Blake went away – never to return again. Now it was all coming out, we were purging ourselves of all the poison, of the things that had been pent up inside us for so long. It should have been done back at Life Works, but it was better late than never.

Unfortunately, while Blake and I were coming to terms with each other, Amy and Mitch were moving away from each other. Almost every day, stories were appearing in the press about a reunion. Blake and Amy made no secret of it, they were going to get back together as soon as Blake was off probation. Mitch didn't like this. He said it would happen "over his dead body". He called Blake a "vampire" and a "liar", a "violent criminal" and a "betrayer".

'I don't care what he calls me, mum. He's just a pain. If he really loves Amy, then he should listen to her.'

The thing is, I'd learned many lessons over the last two years, I'd admitted my shortcomings and laid the blame for Blake's addiction at my own door. I never wanted to lose my boys and I hoped Mitch would never lose Amy, but he was going the wrong way about things. I believed he needed to understand and support her, rather than ranting and raving and using emotional blackmail.

Anyway, Amy was able to sneak away from Mitch and his minders while he was away, promoting himself and his forthcoming record, or on holiday somewhere. She came up to Sheffield to see Blake and stayed for three days and two nights at his flat. They had missed each other so much, and neither Mitch nor I had the right to keep them apart. Amy arrived with two bunches of flowers, a bunch of mixed blooms for Blake and fifteen white roses for me. She was always so thoughtful like that, always doing nice things to make people feel happy.

'It was great when we met, mum. I showed her my new tattoo of a woman with a beehive. Amy looks beautiful. She's like the old Amy I used to know. It was amazing to wake up with her again.'

Amy promised she'd write how it really was between them in her new album, which was due to come out the following year. Blake also wanted to be his own man, not to be thought of as "mister Amy Winehouse", but with his own career either in the music business or the film industry. Amy kissed me when we finally met.

'I'm happiest when I'm with Blake, momsie.'

'I know, Amy.'

'You have an amazing son, who is gorgeous and beautiful and sensitive. But other people don't see it.'

'We see it, my darling. That's all that matters.'

'I love you, momsie.'

'Thank you for the flowers, Amy.'

'I'm glad you like them.'

It was a lovely gesture and it made me feel so happy. But then the media found out she was there and they surrounded Blake's flat. I was worried in case probation didn't like it and sent him back to prison. Amy was still drinking heavily and, after three days, Blake sent her back to London – both for her own good and for his own continued freedom. He was disappointed that someone he trusted told the tabloids Amy was with him. Stories began appearing in the papers. Mitch was furious. One of his "sources" said that Amy had been emotionally blackmailed by Blake to come see him, or he'd self-harm. My son was blasted as a "money-grabbing user" and they said Amy didn't like being blackmailed. What rubbish! How can a man who refused to take a single penny in a divorce settlement be a money-grabber? Once again, the lie-machine was spitting out its vitriolic poison. I worried in case all this would send Blake over the edge.

Probation said they wanted to see him. They gave him a warning.

I was asked to do some interviews about my book and I tried to undo the damage being done by Mitch's statements on Twitter and on television and by his "close sources" in the newspapers. I told people that Blake and Amy were very much in love still and that they would probably re-marry once Blake was clear of licence. I said they had my complete blessing and I just wished that Amy's father would stop trying to prevent the inevitable. At the time, I believed the divorce was the right thing. They needed to step back from each other and take stock of their lives. But now things were different, both Blake and Amy seemed to be more mature and, apart from the drinking, their excesses seemed to be under control. It was going to happen anyway, so why make it more difficult for everybody? Then I thought, was this me giving in to Blake again, just like I did in the old days? Maybe Amy wasn't the best thing for him and maybe he wasn't the best thing for Amy. Maybe Mitch Winehouse was right. It was so difficult to know just what was the right thing. Even though Mitch was slagging Blake off at every opportunity, somehow I knew how he felt. I knew he felt confused, afraid, helpless. But the time comes when you have to stand back, when you have to say to yourself "I've done everything I could – life and fate and the future have to take their own course now. If I continue to oppose these forces, I will only destroy myself and my child forever". Once you accept that, you can find a kind of peace.

Amy began to wear her wedding ring again. I knew neither of them wanted the divorce in the first place, they only did it to please me and Mitch – and the tabloids and the idiots. But they didn't want to pretend any more, they seemed to be meant for each other and there was nothing anyone could do about it.

'We tried to be apart, mum.'

'I know you did, darling.'

'We tried to see other people, but it didn't work. We only want to be together.'

'Then, that's how it has to be.'

'There's no-one like Amy. She will always be the love of my life.'

'Does she feel the same, Blake?'

'Yes, mum. We're both more responsible now. Coming off heroin was hell, but it's alright now .. for both of us.'

I just hoped that, this time round, they'd stay drug-free and they'd have the support of their families to help them work through any problems. I hoped there would be a happy ending this time. I knew Blake wanted children, he was great with the boys and I knew he'd be a wonderful father to his own kids. I knew Amy would be a wonderful mother too – and maybe that's what they needed to steady them, to settle them down, a child of their own, a grandchild for me – and Mitch.

While apart, Amy had been involved in a string of incidents. She was reported as being unruly and drunk at gigs and smashing drinks on the floor and her behaviour was becoming increasingly erratic. She confronted other celebrities and was generally out of order in public. "Sources" described her as being hyper and snarling and she was appearing before magistrates on assault charges. I read stories in the press about her, but I didn't believe half of it as I knew the tabloids were only interested in the negative things and never bothered to print the happy stuff. In the meantime, Mitch became angrier and angrier with Amy for saying she was getting back with Blake when he came off licence. The thought of them getting married again seemed to incense him. It came to a head when she decided to choose Blake over her family for Christmas. Mitch wouldn't allow it. Amy rang me.

'Mitchell and I have fallen out, momsie.'

'I'm sorry to hear that, Amy.'

'He doesn't understand, Blake and I are two of a kind. We share so much .. we have no secrets.'

'I understand what it's like to fall out with someone you love, Amy. Giles and I ...'

'He was lucky to have you, momsie. You're free now.'

'You will be too, Amy.'

Blake was angry about the argument Amy had with her father.

'He shouted at her so badly, mum. He made her cry.'

I was so sorry to hear that. I didn't want Mitch to fall out with his daughter, I just wanted him to let her live her own life.

'"Go see the cunt then", he shouted at her.'

'I don't want to hear, Blake.'

'She told him to fuck off, mum. Then he spat in her face.'

How horrible was that, if it was true? How sad. A father spits in his own daughter's face, just because she loves my son. I'm not perfect, by any stretch of the imagination. I've made so many mistakes – but I would never have done that to my child.

We had a lovely Christmas – myself, the boys, my mother, the whole family! Our journey had been long and painful so far, and we still had some way to go. But we were lucky, we were still together. I called Amy on Christmas Day.

She was alone.

CHAPTER 21
NEW DECADE!
NEW BEGINNING?

Friday brought a new year and a new decade – 2010. I wondered if it would be a new life for Blake and Amy and a new beginning for me. Being with the family over Christmas was truly magic – it had been a long time since we were all as one. But a dark cloud overshadowed the uneasy and fragile feeling of contentment inside me. Blake was using again. He tried to hide it, but I knew it was true – I knew it deep in my heart and it was like a knife cutting through me. I didn't say anything, I wanted to have this time, however short, to be as it used to be, before all the trouble. I wanted to believe the rehab would work – maybe it was just a temporary relapse and it would straighten itself out. But I was being naive, just as naive as I'd been before. I was back to my old trick of denying what was obvious – not facing the facts. But I so much wanted to have faith, to have hope that Blake would at last beat his addiction .

In less than six months, Blake began his descent into darkness again. I felt I was better equipped to deal with it this time, but I still didn't really know what to do. Part of me was angry – we'd been through so much, lost so much, and he was doing it again. Why? Why would he do it to me again – to us again? How could he be so callous. Of course, it wasn't that he was being callous, or wanted to deliberately hurt – it was because he couldn't help it. I prayed for the answer, for guidance – and something told me I had to confront it. Not to pretend it wasn't there anymore. To fight it, you have to face it. I decided to speak to Blake, tell him I knew he was back using again. He didn't deny it.

'I was doing so well, mum .. then this girl came round .. she had gear .. I wasn't strong enough to say no.'

Those words went round and round in my head – "I wasn't strong enough" – "I wasn't strong enough". I knew who the girl was. I spoke to Amy about her.

'Get rid of her, momsie. Blake will never recover as long as she's about.'

The trouble was, Amy was drinking far too much and now Blake was back on the drugs. The situation was impossible.

Some time later, I went to Blake's flat in Sheffield. The flat I'd visited before was beautiful – it had everything he could want. Now it was empty and dirty – all the furniture and equipment like televisions and stereos were gone – sold, to feed his addiction. I hated this girl, who I blamed for bleeding Blake dry, and I wondered if this was how Mitch felt about Blake and, for the first time, I felt a kind of affinity with Amy's father. I suppose we need to blame when things go wrong – we need to blame someone and we rarely blame our own. It dilutes the pain, to have someone else to blame.

In the meantime, Amy was appearing drunk on stage and she was also back in court on another assault charge. This time she was accused of hitting the manager of a Milton Keynes theatre during a pantomime. She pleaded guilty. He refused to serve her any more drink and she pulled his hair and called him names. She appeared at Milton Keynes magistrates court under her married name, Amy Civil, but she didn't wear her wedding ring. She was given a two-year conditional discharge and ordered to pay £100 to the manager and £85 in costs. Her solicitors said the incident had a huge effect on her and she was now curbing her drinking. The judge told her she had to stay on the straight and narrow for two years. Did he believe it would be that easy? Did the lawyers? Did Mitch?

Every time I saw Blake, he looked more ill than the previous time. He was getting thinner and looked a grey colour. Yet he always tried to make me happy, even though he was really making me miserable. Amy was never far away, always there in the background. He loved her and she loved him, but it was impossible for them to be together. The love they felt for each other wasn't enough to control the demons inside them. The media was still witch-hunting – always looking for an excuse to blame him for something. – "junkie this" and "junkie that" – there was nothing he could do about it and nothing I could do about it, so we just tried to ignore it. But they were both on a downhill spiral – both Blake and Amy and there was nothing anyone could do about that either. Then a message was delivered to a pub in Sheffield for Blake. It was supposed to be a message from Mitch Winehouse, asking for a private meeting. I believed it was some kind of stitch-up and I advised Blake not to go. Who knows what might happen, he could be walking into something that would land him back in prison, for a long time. Then a card was delivered to the pub – it said "Leave Amy Alone" and it had "RIP" on the end of it. I was sure someone was going to set Blake up again, just like he'd been set up before. I wanted him to come home.

The telephone rang.

'Mum, I need your help.'

'What's wrong?'

'I need two hundred pounds.'

I could hear a lot of noise in the background, like a door being banged very loudly.

'What's going on, Blake?'

'It's a dealer .. I owe him money. Please pay!'

I did pay. Just like I paid many times before. What else could I do? Unless you have experienced addiction up close and personal, you can never know the level of pain it brings with it. Blake was still with this girl – two drug addicts together, feeding off each other. She'd left her two children behind, to be with him. She told me how much she loved Blake but, surely if you truly love someone, the last thing you would want to do is destroy them? At times I felt like a hypocrite – that was a word Mitch Winehouse had used when Blake was with Amy – now I was using it too. I went over to Sheffield to see Blake again. This time he was in a terrible mess – no food in the flat, he looked like he was going to die.

'Blake, you're coming home with me.'

'No, I'm OK.'

'I'm not leaving till you say you're coming.'

'Only if Sarah comes too.'

Within an hour, we were all on the train back to Lincolnshire. I called Harry to let him know I was on my way back.

'Is Blake with you?'

'Yes, darling, Blake is with me.'

'Is he OK?'

'No, but he will be.'

I had a sense of peace. I thought I could control the situation now that he would be near me. I would protect him from stitch-ups and addiction and everything else the world might throw at him. It was unrealistic, I know. We were on a journey that could only end one way, but at least we were together again. He was my son and I loved him – only a mother can understand that, only a mother's love is unconditional. I knew him like nobody else did – I knew the real Blake, I knew him before he became an addict and I would always love him, with the very last breath in my body. So, we all settled in at home and it was fun being together again – for a while. I had all my boys with me. But it was tough too, having two addicts living together. We got involved with add-action and soon had a methadone programme in place and it looked like we might just make it. Amy rang every day and she was happy Blake was home. She didn't know about Sarah, that was our secret and, anyway, Amy had enough problems without making things worse for her.

In many ways, we were happier than we had been for years and I have some great memories of that time. We were the "secret five" in our little hideaway from the ugly world – like Enid Blyton's "secret seven". But it was a fairy tale that wasn't going to have a happy ending. Before long, Sarah approached a local dealer. She broke the rules and she had to go. Blake stayed – for a while, but he too went in the end.

'Mum, I love you, but I can't desert Sarah.'

'She'll destroy you, Blake.'

'No, she won't. It'll be alright.'

I'd lost the battle. Again. We nearly made it, but nearly wasn't good enough. I went back to my old routine, knowing I'd never win, the addiction would always be the winner – it was too strong for me.

In the summer, Amy was filmed drunk onstage in Belgrade, in front of 20,000 people. She was supposed to be launching her European tour, but she was falling around all over the place and the footage appeared everywhere – on the internet and in the papers and I felt so sorry for her. I wanted to go to her and hold her and help her, but I knew that would be impossible, I'd never get past her "minders" – "minders" who had let this shambles happen, who had allowed her to show herself up in this way. She was booed and jeered and the tour was abandoned. Her "management" said she wouldn't be able to perform to the best of her ability and would go back home. The media said she had no regard for the audience which had paid good money to see her – they said she should go back to rehab and sort herself out. But how could any of them know what was really going on inside her soul? It's easy to wag the finger and be wise.

I didn't see much of Blake for a while, as Sarah didn't make things easy for us to be together. When I was growing up, my father would tease me and say "I hope when you have children, they bring you the same misery you brought me". It was a joke and we both laughed at it, but now it was coming true and it wasn't a joke any more. I longed for that time again, to be a little girl again, to have another chance at life – but I'm sure everybody does at some point on their lives. Don't they? I wondered if I did hurt my dad back then – like Blake was hurting me now. But I was changing as a person. Blake's addiction was making me look at life differently. I might not be able to save him, but I might be able to help others through what I knew – what I'd been through. I woke up one day and thought –

'To hell with it! I don't want to do people's hair any more. I don't want to spend my life trying to make vain people beautiful, when other people need much more basic help.. help to get through the day. Help to keep living'.

So that's what I did. I gave up the salon and went to work in an ex-offender's unit. And I loved it, working with those guys. I treated them with respect and, in return, they trusted me. I saw Blake in every one of them. I saw him every day, in these lost, confused people. I saw him sad and I saw him happy and I tried to help.

After a while, I transferred to a well-known drug-alcohol unit, where I still work. And I became involved with supported housing. I love every minute of it. These people are human beings, with a heart and soul – sure, they made bad choices and now they're lost, but I'm not there to be their judge and jury, I'm there to support them and show them that life can be good and they can come back from the brink. I think if people spared five minutes of their time to talk to one of these unfortunates, they'd see beyond the addict – beyond the alcoholic – to the person. The real person. And, you never know when you or your family might need someone to do the same for you. We all say "It couldn't happen to us", but it could. That's what I said – and it happened to me.

It was a few months later when I got a call from Blake.

'Mum, I'm so unhappy.'

'Come home, please.'

'I can't.'

'You can. Just get in a taxi and keep talking to me. Before you know it, you'll be home.'

'I want to.'

'Please do it, darling. Be with your family. We love you.'

'I'll call you back in a while.'

But he didn't call back. And I didn't hear from him again until Christmas Eve. It should have been a happy time, but it wasn't. I knew Blake was unhappy, so how could I be? It was late in the day when I got a call from a department store.

'Mrs Civil?'

'Yes?'

'We have your son here.'

They put Blake on the phone.

'Mum, I've been caught shoplifting. Will you pay for the stuff?'

'Yes. Put the man back on the phone.'

He'd been caught stealing a sweater worth seven pounds. They said if I paid, they wouldn't bring any charges against him. So I paid.

The next time Blake called me, he was in prison. He'd been caught with a replica gun, after breaking into some premises or other. He had stolen goods in his car and was charged with burglary and possession of a firearm. He was refused bail at the first hearing in Leeds magistrate's court and was remanded to appear before Leeds crown court in April 2011. My heart sank. I knew this would mean another spell in prison and I'd have to go through it all again – the humiliation and the heartbreak of visiting him and seeing how sad he was and I wondered if I'd be able to bear it this time. His voice was low on the other end of the line.

'Can I come home, mum .. if I get bail?'

'Of course, you don't even have to ask that.'

'I'm sorry.'

The nightmare was beginning again. The darkness was coming back. I went over his childhood in my mind – over and over, in minute detail. When did it go wrong? When was it that I failed this boy so terribly? When did he change from the kind, funny, beautiful boy I knew? When did he become so helpless, so hopeless – when did he turn into this person I didn't know – this dark person?

I asked myself these questions.

But I got no answers.

CHAPTER 22
BACK TO BLACK

Blake did get bail and he called me as soon as he could. I didn't go to the court, because I couldn't bear to go through it all over again – the barristers, the judge, the reporters, the vindictiveness and lack of humanity.

'Mum, I got bail. I'm coming home again.'

'Oh darling, I'm so pleased.'

'It'll be just like old times.'

'I hope so, darling.'

'Love you, mum. See you soon.'

He didn't arrive until eleven o'clock that night. But he was happy, full of smiles. It was magic having him back again and I promised myself I'd make it work, no matter what happened at the trial, which would be held in June. My other boys, Harry and Fred, were sceptical.

'How many times have I heard that, mum.'

'I know, Harry, but this time will be different.'

'I hope so. I love him too, but he has to stop the drugs.'

I promised Harry we'd all work hard to help him. Blake was my son, just like him and Fred and I couldn't stop loving him because he was a drug addict. He needed us and we needed him. I felt guilty again, that so much of my love was being manipulated by Blake, to the detriment of my other boys. But I told myself that he needed me most and I'd make it up to Harry and Fred when things got better. But this time there was a difference in Blake that I hadn't seen before. It was as if the heroin had penetrated deeper into his soul. At times I didn't recognise him at all. I knew he was still using and strange people would come round the house at all hours of the day and night. There was one particular family who seemed to be there all the time, even at six in the morning when I was getting breakfast ready. I felt in my heart that they were no good for

Blake and I told him so.

'I'm not happy with these people, Blake.'

'Don't worry, mum, they're OK.'

But every fibre of my being was telling me to try to keep them away. I didn't like them at all. Anyone would think that, after all I'd been through, I'd have been strong enough to tell them to stay away from my son. Yet I didn't. I didn't want to fall out with him and maybe he'd leave the house and go with them. Then I'd have no control whatsoever, not even the little I had now.

Most days, Blake would go out in the morning and stay out until 9:00pm, which was his curfew time. When he came home, he'd be drunk and aggressive and I knew he was using and that there was a strong possibility he'd re-offend. But what could I do? Tell the police? Have him send back to prison to languish there until the trial date? I couldn't do that. I was playing the blame game again, blaming the people he was hanging around with, saying if it wasn't for them –

'Blake, you have to stop seeing these people.'

But there's only so long you can go on blaming others. Eventually I had to admit my son's problem was getting worse, and it would keep getting worse. He was out of reach. I couldn't get through to him. We tried to talk, sitting at the table, sometimes we cried – each of us lost in our own misery. Him locked in the hell of his addiction and me locked in my guilt. I felt so alone. I had wonderful friends, a beautiful family, boys who loved me, a job I loved – yet I felt so alone.

At times I thought, what if I'd done what I planned all those years earlier? Would we all be flying in the sky now? What would it be like? Would Blake be drug-free in heaven? I wondered if Blake felt the same, if he thought sometimes that he'd be better off dead. I wondered what would make him happy.

'Mum, if I had a wish, it would be for Amy to walk through that door, right now.'

Love can be a cruel emotion. It can break you. We all crave it and need it and want it, but it can destroy you, just like addiction. He'd come home late again. He'd been drinking again. The man-boy that stood before me was moving further and further away. I loved him, yet I didn't like him, if you can understand that. I didn't like what he'd become. It was as if someone else had borrowed my son's body and my real son was lost somewhere in the void, in the ether – somewhere I couldn't go and he couldn't get back from.

But it's so easy to feel to feel sorry for yourself – I'd been doing it all my life. Even angry – angry because I loved him and something was taking him away, far away from me. Women I could cope with, prison I could cope with, but not the drugs. That was something that would beat me every time. It was a kind of selfishness and I knew it. But I didn't think I was being unreasonable – he was my son and I brought him into the world and raised him and I had nobody else. Which wasn't true – I had Harry and Fred, but no Giles. I had no strong arm to lean on, no shoulder to cry on. In that respect, I was on my own. Would there ever be anyone else again – another Giles? Another Lance, even? Or would I be alone with the monster – the drug monster – alone to fight it and always lose? I would hug Blake and tell him I loved him, but he already knew that and it made no difference. I no longer made bargains with God – they were all empty promises and He knew it and, anyway, I was tired of it, tired of repeating the same old clichés. Blake had spiralled out of control. He looked terrible and he was facing prison again. I didn't know if I could get through it all again. I just wanted it to end and to have my son back. I wanted what everybody else seemed to have, children who worked and mowed the lawn on Sundays and took their kids to the cinema – normal things. Everyday things.

It was Blake's birthday on 16th April. I went out for a drink with him and we were joined by his "friends". I looked at all these people, the ones who had been instrumental in my son committing crimes, the ones who were encouraging his addiction. They all sat there, laughing, and Blake laughed with them. No-one even gave me a second thought. No-one cared about my misery. I hated them all – even Blake. Something snapped inside me and I couldn't take any more. I had to let go of it all and get away.

I got up and walked out.

Just a little after midnight, I was in bed and was woken up by a commotion. I could hear Harry shouting.

'Harry, what are you shouting about?'

'It's Blake, mum.. he's doing drugs in my room.'

I immediately got up and found Harry outside his room. Blake was inside – shooting up with heroin. He didn't look happy, just so sad. I looked at him and he looked back at me with a kind of pain in his eyes. This was what it had come to, the drug demon had full control and it didn't matter about me or Harry or anybody else. Harry was still shouting.

'I've had enough, mum. I can't take any more of this.'

'Harry, please..'

'No mum, it's him or me.'

It had come down to this, a choice between my two sons – Harry or Blake. I loved both of them. It was a choice I didn't want to make. In any case, the terms of Blake's bail stated he had to live with me. If I threw him out, he'd go straight back to prison.

'Harry, he's your brother..'

'He's a selfish bastard! Get rid of him, mum. Go on, get rid of him!'

I knew it was over, I had to say enough is enough. But my heart was breaking. Blake left that night and a part of me died. I cried for hours.

Sarah was pregnant for Blake and my grandson was born soon after. His mother called him Jack, but I never got to see him. He was addicted to heroin when he was born, through his mother, and had to have treatment. Sarah and I weren't on the best of terms and Blake and I were estranged and she kept him away from me and things were bad between us for a long time – or what seemed like a long time to me. I thought I didn't mind. I was sorry for the boy more than anything else, being born into a world of addiction. I hoped Blake would be a good father to Jack and wouldn't let him down. Being a parent is the hardest job there is, it comes without a rule book and it's difficult at the best of times. But a child born to two addicts? What chance did the poor innocent have? I never was all that good with kids. I find it difficult to relate to them. I love my own children, but I didn't know how I would cope with a grandchild. I wanted to go over to Sheffield and say how much I loved both of them, even if I didn't mean it. But I knew I couldn't. It would be like giving in and saying that what Blake was doing was right. So I stayed away.

Blake was soon back in prison. I didn't go to the court to hear him plead guilty – to hear the sentence – to see his face when they took him down. The same way he looked that first time, three years earlier. The days went by and turned into weeks. There wasn't a single moment when I didn't think about him. I wrote to him, day after day, but he didn't reply to my letters. He obviously hated me.

June became July.

Then the phone rang. It was a reporter and, at first, I couldn't hear what she was saying – something about someone being dead. I panicked.

'What? Blake.. is it Blake?'

'No, it's Amy.'

'Amy?'

'Yes. Amy's dead.'

Oh no! I didn't believe what she was saying. But she went on talking about it being alcohol and did I have any comment. I hung up. I knew Amy was hitting the bottle hard. But Amy dead? All the years came back to me as if they were only yesterday – the pain she brought, and the happiness too. Then I thought about Blake.

'Oh please let him be OK.'

I rang the prison and they told me they would keep an eye on him and not to worry. I prayed to God not to take him too. I cried for hours, until I had no tears left.

But Blake was in the safest place. He'd be alright – for now, at least. I thought about Amy. I'd never be able to talk to her again – never hear her voice again – never hear her laugh. What made her so unhappy? What made them both so unhappy? I wanted to hate her, to blame her, just like Mitch blamed Blake. But I couldn't – I loved her too much. Because she loved him – told the world how much she loved him – wrote songs about him – for him. Her love for him destroyed her, just like his love for her destroyed him. And their love for each other nearly destroyed me.

Dear sweet Amy – I remembered her voice, her phone calls.

'Momsie, out boy is so handsome. I love him.'

My mind went over all the times we shared – the good times and bad.

The tears. The laughter. The love. I wished I could re-write history, but I knew I couldn't. Why did they open the door and allow the drugs in? Could myself and Mitch have done more? I couldn't answer for Mitch, but I felt that I should have.

'Don't cry, momsie. We didn't want to hurt you. We never did it to hurt anyone.'

I wished I could have one more day with her. To tell her how sorry I was and how much I was hurt – not by her, but by such a wasteful world. I knew Blake still loved her, and so did I. I knew he would follow her – how soon, I couldn't say.

But he would follow her.

Like I said, it's easy to feel sorry for ourselves, to feel that life is cruel and vindictive. I know I don't have a monopoly on misery – or addiction. Nor does my son. After Amy died, my attitude changed again. I wanted to learn as much as I could about addiction. I wanted to understand why – understand what it was really like. I thought, if I did that, I might be able to relate to Blake and save him from himself. Amy was gone now, but the addiction was still there and it had to be beaten. I had two other sons, but life without Blake would mean nothing to me. I wondered why my love for him overshadowed everything. What was it about me that made me feel like that? If Blake were to die – so would I.

Blake didn't die in prison and he served half the two-year sentence for burglary and firearms offences. I had very little contact with him during this time – that was his choice, not mine. I wrote to him and requested a visiting order, but he ignored my letters. I didn't blame him, I blamed myself and told myself I deserved it. I cried alone in my bedroom, filled with guilt. But, as the months rolled past, my work helped me deal with my emotions. I started to feel a kind of happiness – an ease of mind. Harry and Fred were happy and we were thinking of buying a house far away – just the three of us. Then, a few days before he was due to be released, I received a card from Blake saying how much he loved me and how he was looking forward to seeing the family again when he got out. I wrote back immediately, telling him I loved him and how sorry I was for the arguments we'd had in the past and how much I was longing to see him. I was working with long-term addicts now and had a better understanding of the problem and how to deal with it. I hoped to be there, waiting for him when he came out, but he didn't let me know. I was at home, waiting for another card to say when he'd be released – and he was already out.

He was free for less than three weeks, when I got a call telling me he was in Dewsbury Hospital, West Yorkshire, in a coma. At first I couldn't get my head round it – what had happened? Why hadn't he contacted me? It was 10:30 in the morning when I got the news and I was at the hospital within two hours. I thought he'd be dead before I got there – I thought he wanted to follow Amy. It was the thing I'd been dreading for years. It was coming true. I was going to lose him – the addiction had won! My heart was racing as I came thought the hospital doors. I couldn't get to his bedside quickly enough. Then I stopped – as I saw him lying there with all those tubes coming from his frail body. The body I'd given birth to and the drugs had ripped away from me so callously. The doctors had put him into a medically-induced coma, to try to save his life and the machine shook his body violently, as if the devil was inside him and he was trying to fight against it. All his vital organs were failing. I was sure he was going to die and this would be my final image of my son. It would haunt me for the rest of my days.

Blake stayed in that coma for twenty days. His life was on the line for those three weeks and they didn't know, if he survived, whether or not he'd be brain damaged. I prayed. I stayed by his bedside and prayed – all that time.

Then, in the third week, he woke and saw me – and smiled. Then we both cried.

The doctors tested his brain and it was alright. He was going to recover. He'd been given another chance – and so had I. But the addiction was still there and it had to be beaten. I vowed I'd do it, if I had to walk every mile with him – every step. If it was the last thing I did on this earth. We were together again. I was beside him again. Only a mother of an addict can know how I felt, the willingness to fight to save your child, when the odds are stacked against you. I knew my boy was a lovely person, deep down inside. He wasn't the monster the tabloids painted him as – all he did was make a bad choice, a choice that would eventually cost him his life. But I had to make a choice now – to be by his side until that happened.

I first thought Blake had tried to commit suicide, to be with Amy. But he told me that wasn't the case. He loved her – he always would, but the overdose was a near-fatal mistake. I hoped this would be enough to shake him up, to make him stop. But would it? I thought about Amy again. She was such a good person, but so full of demons, just like Blake. She lived her own life, after Blake went to prison the first time, yet he's still blamed for her death to this day. It was so unfair – her death and his being blamed for it. But the media love a "bad boy, good girl" story and that's how they wrote it, even if it meant distorting the real truth. Blake told me he read some texts that were on his phone when he came out of prison. He wasn't allowed the phone when he was inside and one of those texts was from Amy – she wanted to be godmother to his son. It was like a voice from the grave and it shook him up so badly he went on the binge. But it wasn't to commit suicide – or so he told me.

Lance Fielder, made a brief visit to the hospital and Blake was glad to see him. Funnily enough, so was I. Our life together was ancient history now and all that mattered was for Blake to make a full recovery. I also saw my grandson, Jack, for the first time. – fourteen months after he was born. His mother brought him to the hospital and I saw him – my grandson – Blake's boy. A beautiful little chap, who smiled at me and I picked him up and I held him and I cried. It was like being given Blake back again. It was like when I first held my son all those years ago. Like a second chance. Jack was Blake and, this time, it would be different. I hugged him and told him I loved him and told him I loved his daddy. I'd tell him all about his daddy one day – the daddy I'd have to bury soon.

Blake was allowed home from hospital – to me. That's where I wanted him, back with me, where I could help him. I had a plan to get him onto a rehab regime. But he wouldn't stay. He went back to Leeds – the most dangerous place he could be, where temptation was all around him.

I've been called many things by the media over the years, and maybe at times I have been outspoken. I make no excuses or apologies for that, it was always in defence of my son, who was being kicked around like a rag doll. What was I supposed to do – shut up and take it? That's not me! As well as what they called me in the media, I was a mother, a wife and a human being, expressing my love for my heroin-addicted son and erstwhile daughter-in-law, during one of the most controversial marriages in showbiz history. I hope I might get through to parents, particularly other mothers, of drug addicts and I hoped it might be a comfort to them to know that someone was sharing their experiences and torments and that someone, at least, understood what they were going through. I just wanted to put things right, to say there are always two sides to every story – a lot was being said and a lot was being left unsaid. I hoped someone would listen.

As the weeks went by, I visited Blake and his family and sometimes he came to stay with me. We were trying to move forward, live each day as it came. But we had no control over what tomorrow was to bring – or the day after that. I knew what my son's fate would eventually be, and it broke my heart. I just wanted him to be happy. I looked at him and I smiled and I loved him. He was my son.

But the time had come when I couldn't do any more for him

When I had to let Blake go.

CHAPTER 23
DENOUEMENT

Because of the work I do, I have great empathy with addicts and alcoholics. They all have their individual reasons for their individual addictions. Over the years, I'd tried to understand what Blake's reason was – what the unhappiness was that put him on the path to where he ended up. I'd gone back and back, right to the beginning – I'd examined every milestone and bump in the road – I'd looked at life from his point-of-view. I'd tried to be him, to see through his eyes. I'd examined my relationship with Giles and my other sons, Fred and Harry. I'd tried everything. In the end, Blake's life was his – and a big part of that life was Amy, not me. She was the most important factor in his life, she was everything and, no matter what I did, I couldn't replace her. Getting to know my grandson, Jack, made me think about Amy – what if she and Blake had had a child together? What would she have been like as a mother? Amy wasn't any different to Blake, she was an addict, just like him, no matter what the propaganda machine said. The one thing that would have been different was money, of course. She could have afforded for someone else to take care of the baby while she got on with her life.

All addicts portray similar traits and Amy was no different. She lied, just as Blake lied. She manipulated, just as Blake manipulated. She was selfish, just as Blake was selfish. But she had a great talent, which made everything sooooo chic. So alright. It's ok to be a junkie, as long as you have talent – we've seen it over and over again in the music industry. You become a commodity, a product, a franchise – something that makes money for other people. I'm not excluding myself from this scenario, I used the newspapers too. I used them to try to tell the world that my son was a good person, not a "junkie scumbag". I lied and lied and didn't even know I was lying and I wonder, if every addict had talent, would there be no more "junkie scumbags"? In the end, Amy wasted that talent and she died without it – a talentless death. A waste. Soooooooooooo sad.

After the coma, I hoped Blake would be able to fight his addiction. I hoped his close encounter with death would be enough to see it off – would give him the strength and incentive to turn things around. I saw Blake as often as I could after he moved back to Leeds. I looked for the signs, hoped for the signs that would tell me he was finally on the road to recovery. And there was one night that was magical, that glowed in the darkness all around it – one night when we all sat together and had dinner like a normal family. We talked and laughed and I dared to hope – for a while. But I soon discovered it was only wishful thinking on my part, he was no nearer to recovery from addiction than he was before the accidental overdose. In some ways he was worse. It didn't take long for his home to become a tip, with more drugs and alcohol than ever. And, in the midst of all this chaos, was my beautiful grandson, Jack – a little boy born to two addicts. What future did he have?

Parents make mistakes, the same as their children make mistakes. We don't know everything, even if we think we do. We have to learn – sometimes the hard way. Looking back now, choosing Giles as Blake's stepfather was a good thing, one of the good things I've done in my life. We loved each other – still do, in our own way. The addiction just got in between us and turned everything upside-down. It muddied the water and we couldn't see the wood for the trees, as they say. Blake's addiction also left scars on his brothers, scars they'll have to carry with them through life. What was once Blake's "problem" became everybody's problem – it escalated and expanded until it swallowed up everything in it's path. We all got "played" in one way or another, to justify the addiction – to account for it – to legitimise it. But it was something that was based on lies, the justification, on fantasy. On self-deception. The more the addiction took hold, the more it needed to be justified, lied about, fantasised and deceived for. Justifying the addiction became a raison d'être – it grew like a cuckoo in the nest, throwing out all reason and rationality.

Then it got to the point where it could no longer be justified – the jus-tification – and reality finally kicked in; after souls had been sold to the devil and the trail of destruction and desolation could be traced back through the years. I looked at my grandson Jack sitting in his little chair, watching TV. That was his only routine, watching TV, while his parents drank and did drugs. And I finally saw through it – the big lie. I saw the beautiful little boy, all innocent and accepting and I finally knew what I was. A coward! For years I'd been justifying Blake – finding excuses for the addiction, assisting it and enabling it. Blaming people – myself, Mitch, Amy, Giles, everybody. But I couldn't do it anymore. I couldn't do this to Jack. He deserved better.

Social Services became concerned that Jack had no social skills at all. Sarah was having a second child for Blake and, on 31st March 2013, she gave birth to a baby girl called Lola. Lola was addicted to heroin through her mother, just like Jack. I saw her a few days later, such a beautiful baby. So Small. So still. As I held her, I knew my journey was coming to an end – my son was an addict and he always would be. I couldn't fight it anymore – I couldn't justify it anymore – I couldn't hope that it would end – anymore.

The following week, I was told that Social Services were placing Lola with foster parents and she wouldn't be allowed to leave the hospital. Blake and Sarah failed to grasp the situation, that their daughter was being taken away from them because of what they were – and possibly their son as well. They failed to understand the reality – failed to accept responsibility. It filled me with sadness and the old guilt came back, the old heart-wrenching reproach that had haunted me for what seemed like forever. I shrugged it off – this wasn't my fault any more. It never was. I looked back over the years, the love and support I gave him – misguided at times, begging and pleading with God, blaming everyone and anyone, fighting, crying, dying inside. The reality of it was, I lost Blake a long time ago – the real Blake. The man I saw before me now wasn't Blake – the man who could put drugs before his own children. That wasn't my son, it was a stranger, someone I didn't know and hadn't known for a long time.

I was wrong to believe I could beat the addiction, that I could somehow outwit it – fool it with lies, with complicity and complacency and self-deception. I knew now it didn't matter, nothing I did would matter in the end. Blake would still walk away from me, despite the pleading and crying, despite the love and lies.

Social Services knew what was going on, even though I'd given urine samples in place of Blake's because he was on probation and I was afraid he'd be sent back to prison. But you only had to look at him and Sarah to know. They decided that Jack was at risk because, when the social worker visited each week, he was always in a chair, watching TV. He was also head banging and was out of control because he had no boundaries – their words. Jack was with Pat, Sarah's mother, while Sarah was in hospital having Lola. Pat was a wonderful person and loved her grandson but, like me, she was powerless in the face of the addiction. A court date was set to decide Jack's future. Blake asked me to give a statement approving an order for Jack to stay with Pat if the worst came to the worst – supporting her as a surrogate mother for the boy. I agreed when he first asked me, but now I realised it was a mistake.

I was having lunch with him and I looked at him across the table. He looked so thin, worse than ever. Jack was with us in a high chair – a beautiful innocent two-year-old boy – and I knew what I had to do. I could feel Blake's pain, even though he didn't know I was going to betray him. But it was him or Jack – I either betrayed my son or I betrayed my grandson. It had to be one or the other and I'd already made my choice. I started to argue with God again, asking Him what he wanted from me – sitting here with a family I was about to destroy – a son I would probably never see again and a grandson who would never know my love. Blake broke into my thoughts.

'Mum ... the court case. Promise me you'll give Pat support. Tell them to let Jack stay with her. Jack and me, we have such fun together.'

'Do you?'

'Yes. I take him to the park. I love him. Please don't let them take him away.'

'Don't you think it's a bit late for that, Blake?'

'I know what they said, but we're having fun. I realise I've been an idiot.'

How many times had I heard that before! I lied again and made a promise. I didn't want a row in front of Jack.

'Have you named me as a possible carer for Jack and Lola, Blake?'

'Of course, but you work. It'll be Pat.'

'If they were with me, you could go into rehab.'

'I will go into rehab, I promise you.'

But I knew he wouldn't. And I knew if the children stayed with Pat, as wonderful as she was, nothing much would change. Blake and Sarah would go round there on the weekends and it would be drugs and drink and the children would be brought up with the addiction – they would be at risk.

'I give you my word, mum. Just promise you'll approve Jack going to Pat's.'

'I promise.'

'Love you mum.'

'Love you too.'

The court case was the very next day. Later, I called the Social Services manager.

'I have to tell you something, Vicky.'

'What's that, Georgette?'

'I've been Blake's enabler.'

'What do you mean?'

'I've supplied urine samples which should have been his.'

There was a silence on the other end of the line for a moment.

'Do you realise what you're saying, Georgette?'

'I'm sorry Vicky. I didn't want him to go back to prison. I'm ashamed, I really am.'

'This is serious, Georgette.'

'I know. I can't give my support for Jack going to Pat either.'

'Why not?'

'She did it too, for both Blake and Sarah.'

I knew that Jack would be removed after the court hearing the next day. He would be taken away. He wouldn't be allowed to stay with me or Pat after what I'd just said.

Social Services had given Blake and Sarah so many chances to sort their lives out – and each time they messed up. This was the final straw. They loved their children, I'm sure of that, but they put drugs first, before everything. That's the nature of heroin, it destroys everything around it, not just the addict.

I was a coward and didn't tell Blake what I'd done. He rang me from the court the next day.

'Mum, I'm begging you ... please don't let them take Jack. I'll do anything ...'

'I'm sorry, Blake.'

'They're reading your statement out ... please, mum!'

His sobbing broke my heart, but I had to stay strong and see it through to the end.

'I'll come home. I'll go to rehab. I'll do anything ... please don't let them take Jack.'

I almost broke. What had I done? I was killing the person I loved more than life itself. I listened to the heartache that was coming through the phone.

'Mum, you're angry. Please don't hurt me like this. Please ...'

'Blake, listen to me, I love you, but Jack deserves better. You know that.'

'Please, ring your solicitor, ring the court, retract your statement.'

I couldn't listen any longer. I hung up. I knew deep in my heart that Jack and Lola would be better off with foster parents than with the addiction. They should be with me, of course, or with Pat – but sooner or later Blake and Sarah would have got round us – the lies and self-deception would have cajoled us.

Lola was kept in the hospital for two weeks. She and Jack were taken away by Social Services on 15th April 2013. They are together, with the same foster-parents.

For people who want to judge, I'd just say this – look at your children and ask yourself if you really know them. Can you truly say they would never do drugs? Are you absolutely certain. If you were in my shoes, what would you have done? I had a normal family once – I had beautiful children and a loving husband and a business. Life was good. Then the devil moved in and, once he had his feet under our table, we couldn't get rid of him. He was never invited and we tried and tried to throw him out – but he was too strong. He wanted our hearts and souls – and he got them. So, all I would say is, don't judge until you've been in the same situation and have come through it – if you ever come through it.

There was a time once, so far back now – Giles and I had a silly row and Blake walked out. I went after him and found him in a bus shelter.

'Are you alright, darling?'

'Yes mum, of course I am.'

'Shall we go get a pizza, just you and me?'

'Yes, lets.'

'Blake, I love you. never forget that.'

'I know, mum. I love you too.'

Blake has cut me from his life for what I did. And I miss him – of course I do. The person he relied on most let him down – betrayed him. That's how he sees it. In his eyes, I took Jack away – and I did. I took him away from the addiction.

I pray with all my heart that Blake makes it. That he will survive and forgive me some day and walk through my door and tell me he's a free man – free of the addiction. But for now I have to let him go. He has to find his own path.

And I have to find peace.

www.apexpublishing.co.uk